"But seek first his kingdom and his righteousness, and all
these things will be given to you as well. Therefore do not
worry about tomorrow, for tomorrow will worry about itself.
Each day has enough trouble of its own."

—MATTHEW 6:33-34 (NIV)

LOVE'S A MYSTERY

Love's a Mystery in Sleepy Hollow, New York
Love's a Mystery in Cape Disappointment, Washington
Love's a Mystery in Cut and Shoot, Texas
Love's a Mystery in Nameless, Tennessee
Love's a Mystery in Hazardville, Connecticut
Love's a Mystery in Deadwood, Oregon
Love's a Mystery in Gnaw Bone, Indiana
Love's a Mystery in Tombstone, Arizona
Love's a Mystery in Peculiar, Missouri
Love's a Mystery in Crooksville, Ohio
Love's a Mystery in Last Chance, Iowa
Love's a Mystery in Panic, Pennsylvania
Love's a Mystery in Embarrass, Wisconsin
Love's a Mystery in Whynot, North Carolina
Love's a Mystery in Burnt Chimney, Virginia

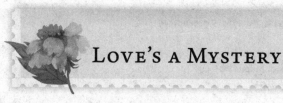

LOVE'S A MYSTERY

in

BURNT CHIMNEY VA

BETH ADAMS &
NANCY NAIGLE

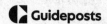

Published by Guideposts Books & Inspirational Media
100 Reserve Road, Suite E200
Danbury, CT 06810
Guideposts.org

Cover and interior design by Müllerhaus
Cover illustration by Dan Burr at Illustration Online LLC.
Typeset by Aptara, Inc.

ISBN 978-1-959634-36-2 (hardcover)
ISBN 978-1-959634-60-7 (epub)

Printed and bound in the United States of America
10 9 8 7 6 5 4 3 2 1

ETERNAL FLAME

by

BETH ADAMS

"When you have eliminated the impossible,
whatever remains,
however improbable,
must be the truth."

—SHERLOCK HOLMES, IN
THE SIGN OF FOUR BY ARTHUR CONAN DOYLE

⌀ CHAPTER ONE ⌀

Rural Virginia

February 1891

Nannie Starkey touched a match to the wick of the kerosene lamp until the flame caught. The days were starting to grow longer again, but the sun still slipped behind the mountains too early, and the dim light from the lamp did little to chase away the gathering shadows. It was nearly time to close up anyway. She rarely had customers this late in the day, and she needed to get home and help Father finish the evening chores. Nannie crossed the shop floor, reached for the poker, and turned to the fireplace. The flames had long since burned down to coals, and she began to spread the ashes around to extinguish them.

The sound of hoofbeats came from the road. Probably someone returning from town. But the sound of the horse's steady footsteps slowed and then stopped outside the small cabin Nannie had converted into a general store. She straightened up and turned around just as the door blew open.

The man who strode in was tall with thick dark hair, deep brown eyes, and refined features. He wore a tailored jacket made of finely spun wool over a starched white shirt and silk vest. Not a farmer, then. There was something arresting about him. Something that made her not want to look away.

"Nannie."

Whoever this stranger was, he knew her name. Who was he?

He was watching her, and for a second, she forgot to breathe. But then his face softened into a small smile, and that was when she knew.

"Everett Turner?" She hadn't seen Everett in years, and it seemed that in that time he'd grown from a gangly, awkward teenager into a man. A very good-looking man, if she was being honest. "I heard you were back in town."

She forced herself to keep her voice even. He might be her old friend, but things had changed since he went away to school. He had become a striking man, but he was still a Turner. His father wanted her family's land badly, and he had already resorted to bullying and threats to try to get it. Everett's older brother, Ned, was more subtle about it, but he had also dropped hints down at the train station over the past few months that if Nannie could convince her father to sell, it would work out well for them all.

"It's good to see you, Nannie. You've grown up."

"That is the way things generally go."

"And you've still got that same feisty spirit. I'm glad to see that hasn't changed." When he smiled, the skin around his eyes crinkled. "And you've really done it. They told me in town that you'd turned your grandparents' old cabin into a general store, but I didn't believe it. I had to see it for myself."

"Yes, well, the cabin was just sitting empty. It seemed like a good opportunity." The cabin had been the first structure on the land, back when her great-grandparents settled here in the Blue Ridge Mountains. They'd eventually built the farmhouse where Nannie's family lived now, and her grandparents had moved out to this cottage just off the road after her parents moved into the main house.

Before Nannie turned it into a store, the small structure had stood empty for years after her grandparents' deaths.

"It's charming." He looked around the space lined with shelves that were stocked with goods folks who lived out this way might need but didn't care to ride all the way to town for. She'd filled the one-room cabin with bins of flour and oats and cornmeal and sugar and salt. Pails of butter and lard and oil sat on the counters next to dried beans and molasses and coffee. She hadn't thought there would be much of a market for eggs, since everyone out here had chickens, and was surprised when the extras laid by the hens in the Starkey henhouse sold well.

She also stocked household items, such as kerosene for lamps, grease for motors, and matches, and ever since she'd started stocking her mother's freshly made cakes and cookies, traffic had picked up considerably. Radcliff's General Store in town had more items and a better selection, but plenty of folks who lived up this way were happy to stop by her store to pick up what they needed instead of going all the way down to Rocky Mount.

The old floorboards creaked as Everett walked around the shop, taking in the jars of preserves and the hard cheese and the side of salted bacon. "You've managed to pack a lot of things into such a small space."

"It's been going well so far." Nannie couldn't keep the note of pride out of her voice.

"I'm glad. It's smart, putting in a shop out this way. And you did it yourself. Who would have thought?"

His words sounded nice enough, but there was a whiff of condescension in the way he said them. As if he couldn't believe she'd managed to do something so clever on her own.

"And you?" Nannie tried to keep the annoyance out of her voice. "You've finished law school?"

Everett had gone east to Charlottesville for college and then up to Boston for law school, as his father made sure to mention regularly. Nannie always burned with jealousy, hearing it. Everett was a few years older than she, so they'd never been in school together, but she'd done well in her classes, and she had a head for figures. She'd always been the cleverest in her year at the old schoolhouse in town, but higher learning was not even considered an option for Nannie. She would have loved to have the opportunity, but going off to college was not a thing women did, even if she could have afforded it.

He nodded. "Graduated early. I couldn't wait to get back home to the beautiful Blue Ridge Mountains. Boston is a pretty town, but there's nothing like our mountains." He stepped toward the fireplace and held out his hands, warming them against the evening chill. The sleeves of his coat rode up, revealing small mother-of-pearl cuff links.

Nannie had to agree. But then, she hadn't really ever seen anywhere else. Farming didn't allow much time for travel.

"And do you plan to practice law in Rocky Mount?" she asked. The only lawyer in town was Jedidiah Hawkins, who had to be in his eighties, but she couldn't imagine there was much need for multiple lawyers in the small town. Lawyers lived in places like Richmond or New York or Washington, DC.

"That's the idea," Everett said. "Working with my dad."

"I see." That explained it then. Robert Turner worked for the railroad, overseeing the station in Rocky Mount. He was also tasked with acquiring land to connect the area with other lines, as had become all too clear in recent years. He had been trying to get Nannie's father to sell their land so he could build a spur to connect Rocky Mount with the line that went through Lynchburg. Having a lawyer working with him could only help his cause. "I'm sure that will prove very beneficial to your father."

"Yes, well, the jury is still out on that. But I came by here today at his request."

"So you didn't come to see my store after all."

"I did, at least partly. Though I was more interested in seeing you." He turned away from the dying embers and smiled at her. "They said you were the prettiest woman in town, and I had to come see for myself."

She knew what he was doing, and it wasn't going to work. "You shouldn't listen to the rubbish they say in town."

"I agree. They were wrong."

"I beg your pardon?"

"They just said you were pretty. No one told me you were absolutely beautiful."

Nannie laughed. Now he was just spitting out flattery. "What is it you really want, Everett? I don't have time to listen to this nonsense."

Everett laughed, but he didn't have the decency to look chastened. "I can see they weren't wrong when they also told me that you wouldn't put up with any games."

"You told me that your father sent you up here. I assume that means he's tasked you with trying to convince me to get my father to sell him the farm?"

"He isn't having any luck convincing your father. He thought I might be able to get through to you."

"And why would he think you would be able to do that?"

"Because we're friends." He gave her a smile that she was sure was meant to be charming. She supposed it probably had its intended effect on women in Boston and Charlottesville. But it wasn't going to work on her. "Remember how we used to play down by the creek?"

Of course she remembered. They'd spent hours down there on the rocky banks while her father picked up supplies in town. Everett's father had been consumed with getting the station built back then and didn't seem to notice when Everett would run down to the creek to play with Nannie. His older brother, Ned, who was supposed to keep an eye on Everett, often got distracted by the daughters of the merchants in town.

"I remember the time you pushed me into the creek," Nannie said.

"Not on purpose." Everett held up his hands. "It wasn't my fault you leaned so far over to gather up those tadpoles. Besides, you managed to pull me in with you. My dad made a fuss when he saw the mess you made of my clothes."

"And yet you always came back. You were there, whenever I went into town."

"That's because you were the prettiest girl around, even back then."

Nannie shook her head and picked up the poker again, spreading the coals out evenly on the brick hearth so they would die out overnight.

"You'll have to talk to my father, I'm afraid. He owns the land. It's been in his family for many generations. It's up to him what he wants to do with it."

"I know that," Everett said. He walked over and stood next to her. "The thing is—and don't take this the wrong way—I've heard from a few folks that things have been difficult over here lately."

"We're managing just fine." Nannie did not need to hear that people in town were talking about them.

"It's totally understandable. It's too much land for one man to farm all by himself."

"He's not all by himself. I help out, and my uncle Gerry over in the next valley helps when he can."

"Your father can't keep up with it all. It's nothing against him. It's just not humanly possible for him to do it alone. Especially with Lenore—"

"You leave my sister out of this." Nannie hadn't meant for the words to come out so forcefully, but the way he stepped back showed her they had.

"Okay, okay. I'm only trying to help," he said, putting his hands up. "Dad heard that your father had fallen behind on payments to the bank. I know he had to take out a loan, what with Leno—"

Seeing her face, he broke off.

"All I'm saying is, no one wants him to lose the farm, Nannie. We all want to help your family. And if selling a few acres would mean keeping the rest of the farm in the family, wouldn't that be best for everyone?"

It seemed like he really did believe it. The thing was, she knew as well as he did exactly who would benefit the most if Father sold the land to the Turners.

"I'm sorry to disappoint you, but I'm afraid things aren't as dire as all that," Nannie said, setting the poker down against the brick fireplace surround. "This store has been bringing in enough that Father has managed to pay down some of the loan, and we'll pay off more soon. He may not be able to farm all the acreage, but with the income from this store, we may not need to anyway."

"Is that right?"

She couldn't tell if it was disbelief or admiration that animated his voice. "You needn't be so surprised."

"I'm not. Well, maybe I am, but—I mean, that's good news."

To his credit, it seemed like he was genuinely pleased for her. Still, she knew better.

"Yes, it is." She lifted her chin. "So it looks like Father won't need to sell the land after all."

"I'm glad to hear it." He forced a smile, though it looked more like a grimace.

She leveled her gaze. "You'll just have to tell your father that he'll need to find some other way to get his railroad built. Now, if you'll excuse me, I need to finish closing up for the night."

"Of course." Everett ducked his head and walked toward the door. "It was good to see you again, Nannie."

She glanced up at him. He really had turned into a startlingly attractive man. The hair, that face, that cocky grin… She could still see the features of the boy she used to play with, but somehow, he had become tall and strong and confident and, well, kind of marvelous.

Still, he was only here because he wanted one thing, and it wasn't something he would ever get.

"See you around, Everett."

He gave her one last smile before he stepped out and let the door fall closed behind him.

Mother was dipping chicken breasts in eggs and breading them when Nannie got back to the house. A pan sat warming on the cast-iron stove, which crackled and popped as the fire inside consumed the wood Mother had used to light it.

"Nannie!" Lenore called when Nannie walked in. Her sister was setting the plates on the table, a task that took every ounce of strength and concentration for her, her little arms moving in tiny spasms the whole time. "Did you sell all of my cookies?"

"I sold a good number of them." Nannie took off her boots, hung her coat by the door, and then made her way across the small kitchen and into the dining nook. Lenore had been born when Nannie was thirteen. Nannie had long since given up any hope of having a sibling by then and, from the beginning, she was almost a second mother to Lenore. The birth had been difficult, and it was clear, even when Lenore was a baby, that something was not quite right. But despite the difficulty of moving her arms and legs, Lenore was a cheerful, happy child.

"Mother said we can make more tomorrow," Lenore said.

"I hope you do." She planted a kiss on her sister's forehead and turned toward Mother. Then she pulled the leather pouch she wore around her neck out from under her dress and dropped the coins into the canister on the piece of butcher block that served as a counter. "Is there anything I can help you with before I head out?"

"No, thank you. Your father needs help more than I do."

"I'll go to the barn as soon as I change."

"Thank you."

Nannie headed up the stairs and into her room. She carefully took off her day dress—a light blue calico with puffed sleeves and buttons down the front—and changed into an old brown dress that was so worn it had become her chores outfit. She had tried to convince Father to allow her to wear pants in the barn, but he had put his foot down. Allowing his daughter to help with the farm chores was bad enough. Letting her do so in pants would be a scandal from which they would never recover. She hurried back down the stairs and pulled on Father's old work boots and her oldest coat before grabbing a lantern and heading out.

Night was falling, and the hills below were lit by the dying sun, row after gorgeous row, stacked one behind the next. Nannie would never get tired of the view, that was for sure. The lamp cast a warm circle of light as she crossed the yard toward the barn. She could just see the little cabin that was now her store across the field. Everything outside the reach of her lantern was hard to make out in the gathering darkness. But the barn door was open, and the glow from Father's lantern told her he was still hard at work.

Father looked up from mucking out the horses' stalls. "Hello."

"Hello," she called. Half a dozen tiny kittens mewled at her as she stepped inside. The barn cat had recently had a litter. She picked one up and stroked its ginger head softly. It tried to bite her hand even as she petted it. "How did things go today? Did you get that fence fixed?"

Even though it was February and too cold to plant the wheat and alfalfa or to start the vegetables in the garden, there was always work to do on the farm. Today Father had planned to fix a broken section of the split-rail fence in the sheep pen. Most families with a farm the size of theirs had a whole brood of boys to share the labor required to keep it going, but her parents had only had two children, both girls at that, and so her father struggled to keep up. Nannie would never have been allowed to help out with the barn chores if Father had any other choice. Most of Mother's time was spent helping Lenore, so Nannie jumped in wherever and whenever she could.

"I got it fixed, thankfully," Father said. "Hopefully, the sheep won't get out again."

"I'm glad to hear it." Nannie could see that Martha still needed to be milked, so she set the kitten down, grabbed a bucket and the stool, and sat down next to the old cow. Nannie and Father worked in silence as he finished tending to the horses. Nannie fed the goats and the sheep after she milked the cow.

"How did it go at the shop?" Father scooped the last of the muck into a wheelbarrow and rested the pitchfork against a wooden post.

"Just fine." There was no need to mention Everett's visit. It would only make Father upset to know the Turners had tried a new tactic to get their land. "Mrs. Meyer bought a big bag of sugar. It seems she burned a birthday cake and needed more quickly. I also sold plenty of nails to Mr. Cooper."

"You were smart to stock what folks in this area might need in a hurry."

"Between that and the baked goods from Mother and Lenore, I brought home enough today to buy us another week or so before the bank comes calling."

"I'm so glad." Father straightened up and smiled at her. "I know I was against it, Nannie—who ever heard of a woman running a store?—but I have to admit I was wrong. That store may be the thing that saves this farm in the end. I don't know what we'd do without it."

All evening, Nannie thought about Father's words, playing them over and over in her mind, and she fell asleep quickly that night. But sometime later, she woke with a start. What was that noise? She sat up as she realized she was hearing something pounding. It took a second for the room to come into focus, but the noise didn't stop. Someone was pounding on the door.

Nannie jumped out of bed and threw a robe over her nightgown. The room had grown chilly, and the floorboards were bitterly cold against her bare feet, but even as she flew to the bedroom door, she could see that something was not right. The sky outside the window had an eerie orange glow. Nannie raced down the stairs but found that Father had preceded her to the first floor and was already undoing the locks on the front door. The pounding stopped as he pulled it open.

"Fire!" the man at the door yelled. "You have to hurry!"

As Nannie rushed to the door, she was startled to see who it was. What was Everett Turner doing at their door?

"Come quick," Everett said. "The store is on fire!"

❦ CHAPTER TWO ❧

Nannie and Father threw on coats and boots, flew out the door, and followed Everett across the yard. Even from here, Nannie could see flames licking the sky through the bare tree limbs. Father started running faster, crossing the yard and the fallow field, but Everett was already ahead of him, rushing toward the burning structure.

By the time Nannie arrived, Everett was helping Father pump water from the old well into a metal bucket. She had never seen Father pump the handle so fast, but she could tell that a bucket of water would make no difference against the roaring fire. The whole structure was already engulfed. Flames licked at the walls and shot through the roof. Shattered glass lay on the ground, glinting in the orange light. The windows had blown out. The roar of the fire sounded like a locomotive pulling into the station, and the smoke was so thick and black it stung her throat.

Father and Everett tossed the bucket of water toward the flames, which swallowed the water up as if it were air. Still, they tried again, working valiantly to save the building, but Nannie just stood and watched. It was too late. There was no way they could save it now.

An explosion rocked the night, and flames shot out of the empty windows in a fiery ball. Father dropped the bucket and pushed Nannie and Everett back. "The kerosene!" he yelled, and Nannie understood. The jars of kerosene she'd stored along the rear wall had just exploded. They moved away, crossing the road to stay safe from the blasts that followed and the roaring furnace before them. Everett's horse was tied to a tree, and he untied the reins and moved the poor, terrified beast down the road, farther from the flames. For a while, Nannie was afraid the sparks that twirled and twisted through the dark sky would ignite some of the surrounding trees, but somehow, they didn't catch. Perhaps the recent snows had saturated the tree limbs and the ground enough to protect them.

There was nothing they could do. She stood next to her father and Everett as they watched all her dreams for her family's future go up in flames. No one said anything for quite a while as the fire danced and spun against the dark night. It was so loud they couldn't have been heard, even if someone had wanted to talk. At some point, what was left of the roof fell in, sending sparks flying everywhere.

Finally, slowly, the fire began to burn itself out, and the rushing flames gave way to a smoldering mess. Only the stone chimney remained, charred and battered, but still standing.

When it was clear the fire would not spread, Father suggested they should get back to bed.

"Thank you," he said to Everett. "For coming to get us and for trying to help."

"What happened?" Nannie asked. "Did you see how it started?"

"No." Everett shook his head. "I was passing by and smelled smoke. I didn't see how it caught—it was already burning by the time I saw it. I rushed to tell you." After a moment he added, "I'm sorry I couldn't do more."

"There was nothing anyone could do," Father said. "Not once it was going like that."

"But something had to have happened to start the fire," Nannie insisted.

"I don't know, Nan," Father said. "We can try to find out more in the morning. For now, I don't think there's anything we can do tonight."

"I'm so sorry about this," Everett said. "Please let me know if there's any way I can help,"

"You already have. Thank you for what you did. You'd better get on home and get some rest."

Nannie was grateful for his help, but she had questions. How could the isolated building have suddenly gone up in flames like that? And the Turners lived in town. Everett had just happened to be coming down this quiet country road right after the fire started? It also seemed astonishingly convenient that only a few hours after she'd told him the store might save them from having to sell the land to his father, he was the one to find the store aflame. Could Father not see how unlikely all these "coincidences" were?

"Actually, I have some questions," Nannie said. "Why were—"

"I'm sorry, I need to get going," Everett said. "I have to see to something."

"We are in your debt," Father said.

Couldn't he see that was exactly where Everett wanted them to be?

Everett nodded, tipped the brim of his hat, and then untied his horse and climbed up into the saddle.

"Let me know if you all need anything," Everett said. He guided his horse back onto the road and started off toward town.

"Come on," Father said. "Let's get some sleep. Things will look brighter in the morning."

Nannie couldn't see how. Daylight was not going to bring the store back.

"The Lord giveth and the Lord taketh away," Father said, his voice choked with emotion. "Blessed be the name of the Lord."

Nannie envied the depth of his faith, that he could praise the Lord, even now.

"Yes, but was it the Lord who took something away this time?" Nannie asked. "Or was it someone else? It doesn't make sense that Everett just happened to be—"

"Your mother is probably beside herself with worry," Father said, a finality in his voice. "We should go back and let her know we're all right."

Nannie knew better than to argue. But as they picked their way over the frosty ground, her mind couldn't stop spinning, wondering again how Everett had ended up being the one to discover the fire.

Something didn't add up about his story. There was something he wasn't telling them.

And Nannie was going to find out what it was.

❦ CHAPTER THREE ❦

When they got home, it was after eleven o'clock. Father explained to Mother and Lenore what had happened, and then Nannie rubbed Lenore's back until her sister fell asleep. Then she went to her room and climbed into her own bed, but the sight of the flames licking at the sky, swallowing her little shop, kept her awake, and she didn't fall asleep until nearly dawn. By the time she woke up, the sun shone brightly and the smell of coffee and fried ham wafted up the steps. Nannie made her way down the stairs but hesitated when she heard Mother and Father talking in quiet whispers.

"—maybe it's a sign that it's finally time to sell," Mother was saying.

"I'm not selling the family farm. My great-grandfather settled this land, and I'm not going to be the one to ruin it by letting the railroad through."

"They might not even be able to bring the railroad through, not unless they can get that piece of land the old schoolhouse is on. And you could sell the western quarter and still have plenty of land to farm."

The western quarter was not being farmed anyway, but Mother was too kind to point that out. They simply didn't have the help to farm all that rich land. Nannie felt bad hovering on the stairs, listening to her parents' conversation like this, but she wanted to know what Father would say.

"But if they are able to get the schoolhouse and this land, they would bring the railroad through before you could turn around," Father said. "And this quiet piece of paradise would be spoiled."

"You may not have much choice soon, especially without the money the store was bringing in," Mother said.

"The Lord works all things for good. He will provide," Father said, and there was a finality in his voice that even Mother dared not argue with.

Nannie decided it was time to announce her presence. She continued down the stairs and stepped into the living room. As she did, she overheard Mother quietly say, "Make sure she understands it's not her fault. That fireplace has always been problematic—"

"Good morning," Nannie said, and both of her parents looked up and smiled. Father wore his work clothes, and Nannie guessed he'd already been out to the barn. "I'm sorry I slept so late."

"I'm glad you did," Mother said. "You needed it."

"Good morning, Nannie."

She turned and saw Lenore resting on the settee.

"Good morning, 'Nore. Did you get back to sleep all right?"

"I did." Lenore nodded. "And don't worry, I agree with Mother. You shouldn't feel bad about the old fireplace burning the shop down."

She knew that was what Mother had implied in her earlier comment, the one she wasn't supposed to hear, but it still stung to hear it spoken so plainly. They thought the fire had started because she hadn't extinguished the coals in the fireplace thoroughly. Nannie knew that wasn't the case. It couldn't be.

"I'm not so sure that's what happened, 'Nore." She wouldn't cast aspersions on Everett, not here anyway, but today she would try to find out more about how that fire *really* started.

"Mother says it's not your fault," Lenore continued. "She said that one time the same thing almost happened to Grandpa and if he hadn't been there and caught it right away, it would have burned down then."

"I don't know if that's how it—"

"Let's eat." Mother set a plate of griddle cakes onto the table with a *thunk*. "And thank the Lord for this new day."

Nannie knew the subject was closed. But that didn't mean she was convinced.

After breakfast, Nannie rushed through the remaining chores, feeding and watering the cows and horses and chasing the goats and sheep out into the pens. Then, while Father hitched up Longford to the plow and headed to the fields, she walked across the yard toward the remains of her store. It was so strange to see a pile of ash instead of the small structure that had been there her entire life. Seeing it now, in the daylight, brought tears to her eyes. There was nothing but charred wood and a few blackened beams and that stone chimney, burnt but still standing. It looked completely out of place there on its own.

She hitched up her skirt and stepped into the mess, careful to avoid the few pockets where hot coals still smoked. Had this all happened because of a spark from the fireplace? She gingerly made her way over to where the fireplace stood. Had a burning ember shot out of the ashes and onto the floor? She couldn't see how it was possible.

Nannie kicked aside a pile of charred wood and found the cash register beneath. Its brass shell had turned black, and the glass display was shattered, but it had managed to withstand the flames. She carefully picked her way through the ashes, looking for anything that remained or anything that could give her a clue as to what had truly happened. She found the wooden door of the shop, blackened and marked, but somehow intact in places. Pieces of a broken kerosene bottle and jars of preserves littered the ground. And there in the corner, so small she almost missed it, was a—

Wait a moment. Nannie nudged the object with her toe. A bit of the black char rubbed off, and the gold beneath glinted in the sun. Nannie bent down and reached for it. It was cool enough to touch, so she picked it up. It was a cuff link. A round, gold cuff link, with something engraved on its surface. She brushed off more of the black powder. The letters *ET* were pressed into the gold.

ET.

Everett Turner.

Nannie clutched the cuff link tightly. This was it. Everett must have dropped this last night. He had to have dropped it before the fire started. Nannie felt herself growing more certain as the puzzle pieces fell into place. Here was proof that he was inside the store before the fire started. This was proof that he had set the fire, just as she had suspected!

Nannie held the cuff link tightly as she ran back toward the house. "Father!" she shouted as she got closer. "Father, guess what I found!"

Mother stepped out the side door, a dish towel in her hands. "What is it, Nannie?"

"I found something I need to show Father," Nannie cried.

"He's out in the rear quarter," Mother said. "What is it?"

"It's a cuff link, imprinted with the initials ET," Nannie said. "It's Everett Turner's. It proves he set the fire!"

Mother cocked her head. "Didn't you say Everett came to the shop yesterday afternoon?"

"Yes, he—"

Oh. Oh right. Now Nannie saw what Mother was suggesting. "He did," Nannie said. "But he didn't drop this then. He had on different cuff links. Those were mother-of-pearl, and this is gold."

"Are you sure?" Mother twisted the towel in her hands.

"I'm sure." Besides, Nannie still couldn't believe that he had just happened to be coming down the road when the fire started. That was too much of a coincidence for anyone to believe. He had set the fire and dropped his cuff link in the process.

Nannie made a decision. "I'm going to see the sheriff," she said.

"Don't you think you should wait for your father to come back?" Mother asked.

"No." There was no time to waste. "No, I'll go now. The sheriff will need to come out and investigate, and the sooner he gets started the better."

"I think you should wait and talk to your father," Mother said, but Nannie was already heading for the barn. She wasn't going to just sit around and wait. Father would be out in the fields all morning, and after lunch he might not want to take the time to go into town. Nannie made the short jaunt on her own all the time. Some people thought it was inappropriate for a woman to ride even that little distance without a man by her side, but those were the same people who thought a woman couldn't run a shop on her own, and she didn't listen to them. She threw open the barn door and led Kildare out of his stall.

"Are you ready for a trip to town?" she asked as she patted the roan horse named for the county her great-grandfather had emigrated from so many years ago.

Kildare nickered and blew out a breath. Nannie saddled him and slipped the bit into his mouth. She often hitched up the wagon when she went to town so she could bring back supplies, but she didn't plan to buy anything for the house and she didn't need anything for the store at present…

She banished the dark thought and climbed into the saddle. She'd tell the sheriff about Everett, and once he'd been arrested for the fire, the Turners would have to pay for her to rebuild. Everything would be all right. After she was settled, she clicked her tongue, and the horse started off. It was only a couple miles to town. Usually, it took her less than a half hour to descend the winding mountain road. It would be even faster if she could ride with a normal saddle, but she was stuck using a sidesaddle. There were certain lines even she knew she couldn't cross.

Still, Kildare's steps were light and quick. The road curved around the hills, and the cleared farmland gave way to trees and then, slowly, to the wooden buildings that made up the outskirts of the small town of Rocky Mount. Nannie passed the old, abandoned schoolhouse that had been replaced by a newer one, built in the middle of town a few years ago. She passed the rail yard, the train station, and the Turner & Sons office, where Robert Turner managed his little empire. Then the main street came into view, lined with brick storefronts. She passed the milliner's, the haberdashery, and the cooper's. When she was in front of the blacksmith shop, Earl Miller stepped out and blinked into the bright sun.

"Good morning, Miss Starkey," Earl said. Earl's speech wasn't slurred yet, so that was better than most days. Earl worked at the rail yard on line repairs, and today he wore his traditional uniform of dirty overalls and a torn work shirt under a heavy canvas jacket. His hat was cocked to the side. He'd come to the area ten years ago to help build the train tracks, and it was common knowledge that he had a still out behind his cabin. He was a fixture in town. "I hear there's been some trouble up at your place?"

"You could say that." Nannie stopped her horse. Earl had expressed his strong conviction that women shouldn't run businesses—that it was improper—on many occasions. It seemed to Nannie that he had a lot of opinions about how people should behave for a man who spent a lot of his free time at the new saloon down the road from the Starkey farm.

"Maybe now you'll come to your senses and get married," Earl said. "Without that shop distracting you."

"Maybe." Nannie kept a smile frozen on her face.

"Plenty of good men in this town looking for wives," Earl continued. "Makes no sense for a woman to waste her time with a shop when a husband could be providing for her."

It took everything she had to keep smiling. "Have a good day, Mr. Miller," she said before she nudged Kildare.

Earl mumbled something under his breath and started walking toward the rail yard. Nannie kept going the other direction, and when she reached the town hall, she slid off the horse and tied up Kildare at the hitching post. The town hall was the tallest building in Rocky Mount—three floors plus an impressive facade and with a pretty brick exterior—but Nannie hadn't ever been inside. Father handled all of the municipal business.

She turned up the wooden walkway and entered through the wrought iron and glass doors. Every head in the large open room swiveled as she walked up to the man at the front desk.

"Hello, I'm here to see the sheriff." Nannie made her voice as steady as possible.

A man at the nearby counter answered. He wore a suit and tie and had a stack of papers in front of him. "You here by yourself?" Nannie didn't know who he was, but she recognized the man at the desk behind him—the one who was craning his neck to get a look at her—as the man who collected the taxes.

"That's right," Nannie said. "And I need to speak with Sheriff Bush."

"I'm not sure if he's available," the man said. "He's very busy, you know."

Nannie found that hard to believe. The sheriff's job consisted mostly of keeping drunks off the streets.

"Could you please find out?" she asked.

The man sighed loudly. She stood there awkwardly while he went into another room. The other two men kept casting glances at her but ducked their heads whenever she caught their eyes.

"He's back here," the man finally called. He gestured for Nannie to come through the main room. She followed him down a hall and found herself in a small office across from the metal cage that served as a jail.

The sheriff was a large man with a white shirt and burgundy vest pulled taut over his protruding belly. He nodded but didn't rise when she walked into the room. He gestured for her to sit in the chair across from his desk.

"What did you need to talk to me about, little lady?"

Nannie ignored the infantilizing tone in his voice. "My name is Nannette Starkey."

"Ah. You're Alexander's daughter."

"That's right, sir.

"He couldn't come with you today?"

"I'm afraid he couldn't."

The sheriff's eyes narrowed, but he didn't comment.

"There was a fire out at our place on Rocky Ridge Road last night about ten o'clock."

"I heard about that," he said, leaning forward. "That little house on the corner?"

"That's right," Nannie said. "It's now a store. Or, well, it was. But it burned down last night, and this morning I found this in the ashes." She pulled the cuff link out of the little pouch she kept in her coat pocket. "Last night Everett Turner was the one who alerted us to the fire, and I thought it was strange because he had no business being out that way. But then when I found this inside the store, I understood. It was covered in soot, so it must have been there before the fire. I think he must have dropped it when he broke in to set the fire."

Sheriff Bush blinked but didn't move. Finally, he sat forward. "That's quite an accusation, Miss Starkey."

She held out the cuff link, and he took it and turned it over in his hands.

"I know that, but you see, the Turners have been after my father's land, and just yesterday, only hours before the fire, I told Everett Turner that the store was bringing in enough money that Father wouldn't have to sell. Then, only a few hours later, Everett was there at the scene of the fire, and this morning I found his cuff link. It's a little too perfect to be coincidence, don't you think?"

Sheriff Bush let out a long sigh. "But you just said Everett was the one who alerted you to the fire. Why would he set your store on fire and then come and tell you about it and help you fight it?"

"So we wouldn't suspect him, obviously," Nannie said.

"But you just said he had no business being out by your place. Why would he make his presence known at all? Why wouldn't he simply light the fire and get out of there?"

Nannie didn't have an answer for that, but there had to be one. "I guess you'll have to ask him."

"Why are you so sure he dropped it before the fire started? Why couldn't he have dropped it when he was helping you fight it?"

"Because I found the cuff link in the store, not outside. The fire was raging so strong when we got there, none of us even thought of going inside."

"How can you be sure this cuff link belongs to Everett Turner?"

"The initials on it are E.T. Who else could it be?" She shrugged. "You can ask him to see the matching one. I bet he has it."

"Even assuming you're right, which I think is still a stretch at this point, how do you know he dropped it last night? He could have dropped it earlier than yesterday, and you just didn't find it until now."

"The only time Everett Turner has ever been in my store was just as I was about to close up for the day yesterday, and he was wearing mother-of-pearl cuff links then."

"So you're saying Everett Turner wore one set of cuff links yesterday evening, and then he went home and—let me make sure I get this right—changed into different cuff links before breaking into your store to set the fire?"

"He must have."

"Did he change anything else about his outfit between his visit to the shop and the fire?"

"I don't know," Nannie said. "He wore a coat."

"And the cuff link fell out...through his coat?"

"It could have slipped out of the sleeve." Why was he arguing with her? Why couldn't he focus on investigating Everett?

Sheriff Bush sighed. "You're aware that the Turners are a very powerful family in this town?"

"I am, sir. But that doesn't matter, does it? The truth is what matters, and the truth is Everett Turner set fire to my store."

Once again, the sheriff sighed. "How about this? I will talk to the Turners and see what Everett has to say." He held out the cuff link, gesturing for her to take it back.

Nannie wanted him to do more than that. She wanted him to rush out and arrest Everett right away. But she nodded. "Thank you," she said, taking the cuff link and pushing herself up. She wasn't confident he had taken her seriously, but he'd said he would talk to Everett. She would just have to hope he would see the truth as clearly as she did.

Nannie felt three pairs of eyes on her as she walked across the main floor again, and when she stepped outside, she turned left and headed toward Third Street, where Molly Campbell lived. Molly's father owned the First Bank of Rocky Mount, and he had recently built a grand home in the latest fashion, dripping with gingerbread trim and adorned by cornices and molding.

But just as she was about to turn onto Third Street, Nannie saw Molly step out of the milliner's, a bundle tucked under her arm. Molly wore a yellow silk frock trimmed in ribbons and lace, and her hair was twisted up in a fashionable new style. Despite all the trappings that her father's wealth afforded her, Molly was very down-to-earth, and she was Nannie's closest friend.

Molly saw Nannie and waved. "Nannie!" she called. Mrs. Campbell, a step ahead of her daughter, frowned at her disapprovingly. Molly had the good grace to look contrite, but she hurried toward Nannie nonetheless. "I'm so glad to see you," she said when she got to her. She slipped her free arm through Nannie's and steered her back down Main Street. "They're saying there was a fire at your store last night. Is it true?"

"It is true, I'm afraid." Nannie's voice hitched. She was glad they were walking, as it gave her something to do besides cry. "It's—it's gone."

"I'm so sorry," Molly said. "Was anyone hurt?"

"No. Thankfully, no one was hurt." Nannie shook her head and fought back more tears that threatened to rise up. "It was the middle of the night. No one was there. But the store is totally ruined. I came to town to let the sheriff know Everett Turner set the fire."

"Everett Turner?" Molly lifted an eyebrow. "Why would he do that?"

Nannie told her about Everett's visit to the shop, about his waking them to tell them about the fire, and about finding the cuff link. Nannie expected Molly to raise the same questions Mother and the sheriff had, and Nannie was prepared with her answers, but instead, Molly said, "I've seen Everett around. He's grown up, hasn't he?"

"I guess?" What did that have to do with anything?

"He's very handsome," Molly said. "Of course, Teddy is better looking, but Everett Turner does give him a run for his money."

Teddy was the senator's son Molly was engaged to marry. She would be moving to Richmond after her wedding in June.

"Except that he burned down my shop."

"You don't know that."

"Didn't you hear what I said? He had no reason to be out by our place last night."

"Actually, there could be a simple explanation for why Everett would be on Rocky Ridge Road late at night," Molly said.

"What is that?" Nannie cocked her head.

Molly pursed her lips. "Really, Nannie. You know as well as I do about Hanson's."

Hanson's was the new tavern and inn that had opened half a mile down the road from the Turner farm, housed in the old Theobald place after the family moved on. Nannie had only heard it mentioned in whispered tones, but she knew Father was upset about it. She thought it was a silly location for a tavern, being so far from town, but the town council had fought successfully to keep the sordid business outside the city limits.

"Do you really think he'd come all the way out past our house for a drink?" Nannie asked.

"Or for the gambling tables," Molly said. "I've heard they have those there as well."

Nannie considered this. It did seem plausible. Still, the tavern sat at the corner of Rocky Ridge Road and Hillcrest Road, and Hillcrest was a more direct path from town.

"But if he'd been headed to Hanson's, why wouldn't he take Hillcrest? That would get him there quicker. He still had no good reason to be on our stretch of Rocky Ridge."

"I don't know. And I'm not saying he couldn't have set it," Molly continued. "I'm just saying there may be a legitimate reason he was riding down Rocky Ridge Road late at night."

"I wouldn't call going to a saloon legitimate."

"Well, you're right about that. But the point is, it does mean he might have had a reason for being out your way."

"If that was his reason, then he's changed," Nannie said, shaking her head.

Whatever Molly was about to say was swallowed up by someone calling out from across the street. They'd strolled all the way to the far end of the main street and were in front of Radcliff's General Store. Frank Radcliff must have seen them and come out to say hello.

"I heard the news about your shop, Nannie," Frank called. "I'm so sorry."

"Thank you, Frank." Frank had a pleasant face and a ready smile. His father had started the general store back when the train station had put Rocky Mount on the map. Frank and his older brother Jimmy had grown up helping their father and now worked alongside him. He'd always been kind to Nannie, and in the past few months, he'd been paying special attention to her. She wasn't interested in Frank in that way but thought it was pretty decent that he'd continued to be kind to her even after she'd opened her own shop in direct competition to his.

Molly waved and started walking toward Frank, and Nannie, her arm still linked with Molly's, had to go with her.

"I'm terribly sorry to hear about it. If there's anything you need, please let me know," Frank said.

"I appreciate it, and I will." Nannie tried to subtly steer Molly away and continue their walk, but Molly stepped forward.

"Why Frank, you've hurt yourself," Molly exclaimed. Nannie looked up and saw that Molly was right—when he'd lifted his arm, his sleeve had ridden up, and there was a bandage on his wrist.

"It's nothing." Frank quickly pulled the sleeve down. "Just a cut. I caught it on the edge of a barrel."

Nannie hadn't realized barrels had such sharp edges. "I hope it heals quickly," she said with a smile. "Now, we must be going." This time she not-so-subtly turned, and Molly had to follow.

"Have a great day!" Molly called jauntily before turning back to Nannie.

"I don't see why you can't be kinder to him," she said as soon as they were out of earshot.

"I was perfectly nice."

"You know what I mean." Molly gave her a look.

"I don't want to encourage him."

"Why not?" Molly shrugged. "You could do a lot worse than Frank Radcliff, you know. He's a good man. He's from a good family. You could close your shop and go to work with him at his. In some ways, it couldn't be more perfect."

"In other ways, though…"

"So maybe he's not the most handsome or charming man in town. There are other things that are more important."

"Says the woman with the charming, handsome fiancé."

"Teddy is pretty great," Molly admitted. "But Frank would be a good match for you. What do you have against him?"

"He's so… nice."

"You say that like it's a bad thing. A nice husband is a good thing. Plus, if you won't come with me to find a rich husband in Richmond—"

"You know I can't leave Lenore."

"I could introduce you to some of Teddy's friends. You'd be a big hit in their circle."

"I can't move to Richmond, Molly."

Molly was undeterred. "Then you'll have to find someone local, and Frank wouldn't be a bad option."

"I'd spend my days biting my tongue, trying not to say something horrible about how blandly pleasant it all is."

"Again, pleasant is not a bad thing."

"No, thank you. Besides, I don't want to work at his store."

Molly looked like she was going to say more, but she closed her mouth. They continued walking up the street, but there was a strange expression on Molly's face.

"What is it?" Nannie said. "You want to say something."

"Well, please don't take this the wrong way," Molly said.

"I can't promise that," Nannie said. "But I will love you anyway."

"I wonder if… Well, if things have changed now, with what's happened. I wonder if maybe, with the shop gone, it might be smart for you to start thinking about your options."

"The shop is not gone," Nannie said. "This is temporary. I'll rebuild and open it again."

Molly pressed her lips together. "I'm glad to hear that," she said. But then she added, "It's just—I'm not sure how you plan to do that."

She meant because there was no money to build a new shop and fill it with inventory to replace what she'd lost. But Nannie had her answer all ready. "That's why I need to prove that Everett started the fire," she said. "Once I prove that, he'll have to pay to make it right."

Molly didn't say anything. But she looked dubious.

Well, she would see. Nannie would show them all.

CHAPTER FOUR

After she said goodbye to Molly, Nannie climbed onto Kildare and turned toward home. She thought about what Molly had said—and hadn't said—as Kildare plodded along the dirt road through town. Molly knew the Starkeys didn't have the money to rebuild the shop. Molly had never come out and said it, but Nannie suspected that the fact that her friend's father hadn't yet foreclosed on the mortgage on the Turner land was because Molly had begged him to be lenient. The shop was the only thing that had kept Nannie's parents from having to sell. She had to find a way.

"Hello, Nannie!" someone called.

Nannie turned and saw Ned Turner step out of the railroad office and hurry toward her. Ned was Everett's older brother, but he had a more boyish face, lighter hair and eyes, and a more cheerful demeanor. Ned managed a lot of the day-to-day tasks around the station, including the transfer of goods from the train. Nannie's heart sank when she saw him. Suddenly she remembered what day it was.

"Your shipment of goods for the shop came in on the morning train," Ned said.

Once a week, a shipment of staples—flour, sugar, beans, lard, fuel oil—arrived on the train from a supplier in Raleigh to stock her store. Today was the day she should have come to town with the buckboard to pick up the shipment and bring it back up the hill, but in all the excitement, she'd forgotten. More to the point, she no longer had a store to sell the goods in.

"I apologize. I'll —"

But Ned held up his hand. "I heard about the trouble up at your place. I'm sorry, Nannie." She could tell how deeply he meant the words. "Everett said the store was a total loss."

"All that's left is the chimney," Nannie said. Secretly, she wondered what else Everett had told him, but she couldn't ask—not right now, anyway. She couldn't let Ned know her suspicions about his brother.

"I'm sorry to hear that. And look, I know it's not typical, but if you need us to hold on to your shipment here for a little while, we can do that."

"Thank you, Ned." That was a very generous offer, but what to do with the things that had come off the train was only part of her problem. She still had to pay for that shipment, whether or not she had a store to sell it in.

"And we do plenty of business here at the station with that supplier," Ned continued. "I can see if we can call in a favor and buy some time before your payment is due, if that's helpful."

"That would be wonderful, Ned." Nannie let out a breath. "You'd really do that for me?"

"Of course. You've had some rotten luck. It's the least we can do."

Nannie was pretty sure it wasn't just rotten luck, but he didn't know that, and she appreciated his generosity.

"Thank you, Ned." Why couldn't Everett be more like his brother? She could see Everett through the glass panel of the office door. He sat there, gazing out at her, a strange look on his face. "I can't tell you how much I appreciate it."

Nannie was about to nudge Kildare to start up again, but she had another thought. Ned might not be willing to talk about what his brother had been up to the evening before. But then again, she'd never gotten the sense that the brothers were especially close. It couldn't hurt to ask him.

"Ned, can you think of any reason Everett would have been out on Rocky Ridge Road last night?" she asked.

"I have no idea, and I didn't ask him. Marjorie and I went to bed early," Ned said. "She's so tired these days." Marjorie was his wife, a beautiful but frosty woman who was about to have their third child. They lived in a house just down the road from Molly. Nannie assumed Everett lived in the Turner house with his father now that he was back in town.

"I was just curious," she said, changing her mind about pressing the issue. No need to get Ned mixed up in this. Hopefully, the sheriff would do his job and this would all be settled soon anyway. She thanked him again and cast one last glance into the office. Everett was still watching her, looking as if he'd seen a ghost.

She nudged Kildare and headed back home. As she continued up the road that led out of town, she thought about how, even though Ned was a Turner and would profit immensely if Father ended up selling the land to the railroad, he had never rooted for her downfall. He'd always treated her kindly and helped load her weekly shipment, making sure she had everything she needed. If he thought it was odd that a woman ran a business, he never showed it.

When Nannie got back to the farm, Father had already eaten lunch and returned to the fields. Nannie assisted Mother with the wash and then helped Lenore, who was kneading bread dough.

"Nannie, if I tell you something, will you promise not to be angry with me?" Lenore asked. She knelt on a chair and kneaded the dough, pressing it down against the oiled wood counter. This was a task Lenore enjoyed, as it didn't require precision.

"Of course," Nannie said. She couldn't imagine what her sister could have done that would make anyone angry.

"Last night, when I was supposed to be asleep, I was awake," Lenore said. "I didn't mean to be up, but I…" She let her voice trail off.

"What is it, Lenore?"

"Well, you know those kittens in the barn?"

"Yes." Nannie had a feeling she knew where this was going. Lenore adored those kittens.

"I know Father said not to bring them inside the house, but the littlest one, the calico, well, the other kittens pick on her, and I didn't want her to be upset. I named her Muffin."

Nannie stifled a smile. "Did you bring Muffin into the house?"

Lenore nodded sheepishly. "I kept her in my room last night. I just wanted to keep her safe."

"Barn cats are wild," Nannie said. "They don't belong in the house." She repeated the words their father had uttered many times.

"I know, but Muffin is just a baby. And she's so cute."

"Those kittens are cute," Nannie said. "I can't deny that. But I hope you were careful. You could get badly scratched."

"Oh, I'm careful. I put her back in the barn first thing this morning." She paused. "Anyway, I wanted to tell you this because, well, I was awake late last night playing with Muffin when I was supposed to be asleep, and I think I might have seen something."

"Something like what?" Nannie's heartbeat sped up. Now she understood why Lenore was telling her this.

"I didn't see anyone start the fire. But I looked out the window, and I did see a man in a bowler hat riding past the house a little bit before Mr. Turner pounded on our door. I don't know if it was the man who started it, but I thought I should mention it, just in case."

"A bowler hat?" Half the men in town wore bowler hats. "Could you see anything else about him?"

"No," Lenore said. "Just that the hat was light-colored and had a dark ribbon around it."

A light hat with a dark ribbon. Where had she seen one of those recently?

"I wish I could have seen more about him," Lenore said. "But I thought I should tell you."

"Thank you, Lenore. I'm glad you did."

"You won't…" Lenore punched the dough down with her fists. "You won't tell Father, will you?"

"About Muffin?" Nannie tried to keep her face straight. "No, I won't tell Father. Your secret is safe with me."

"Thanks, Nannie."

After the dough was set to rise, Nannie hauled water from the well, heated it on the stove, and then poured it into the old metal tub so Lenore could enjoy a hot bath, which helped with the pain in her legs. As she soaked, Lenore chattered away, telling her about the kind of man she planned to marry someday—he would be handsome, and rich, and kind, and they would live in a big house in town. Nannie asked questions about the man's occupation and how they would decorate the house and how many children they would have. Nannie knew the chances were slim Lenore would ever marry or live away from her family, but she saw no reason to spoil her little sister's dreams by telling her so.

That evening, Nannie went out to the barn to help with the chores. Father had come in from the fields and was milking Martha.

"Hello there," Father said, looking up. "I hear you went to town earlier."

"That's right," Nannie said. "I wanted to show the sheriff the cuff link I found in the ashes this morning."

"Your mother mentioned that," Father said. "I'd like to see it."

"All right," Nannie said. "It was inside the building, covered in soot."

"Once we get done here, why don't you show me?"

After the cows were milked and the horses and chickens fed, Nannie fetched the cuff link and walked with Father across the muddy yard. The sun had slipped behind the hills, and the light was already starting to disappear from the sky. Nannie knew they didn't have much time before it was fully dark. Night fell quickly this time of year. She gave the cuff link to Father and showed him where in the ashes she'd found it. Bits of the rubble still steamed, and they carefully picked their way through. Father looked at the cuff link in his hand and then down at the ground. He walked around, searching for... Well, she didn't know what. When he got to the door, which lay a little ways outside the footprint of the building itself, he knelt and rubbed his fingers over the wood. They came away black, covered in soot.

"What is it?" Nannie asked.

"It's strange, how the door is over here, apart from the rest of the building," Father said slowly. "And how it didn't burn up, like everything else."

"It is odd, isn't it?" Nannie said. She didn't want to get her hopes up, but it almost seemed as though Father was reconsidering his assumptions about how the fire started. "It would have burned like the rest of it if it had been attached to the building, wouldn't it?"

Father nodded. He ran his fingers over the wood once more and then leaned forward, squinting at something in the dying light.

"What is it?" Nannie asked.

"I'm trying to figure out what these marks are," Father said. He pointed at a section of the door just under the top hinge, where slivers of wood had been scraped away. "Was it like this before?"

"No." Nannie knelt and studied the wood, and she shook her head. "No, it wasn't." She felt a surge of hope. It looked almost as if—

"I'm guessing the door was pried open," Father said. He ran his fingers along the door and brushed away the soot around the lower hinge. There were similar marks there. "Using a claw bar, or something like it."

"It would explain why the door wasn't attached to the frame anymore," Nannie said. She couldn't help the surge of hope that rose in her. Father believed her. "If someone pried it open and tossed it aside on the way in."

Father nodded again. Slowly, he straightened up. "I'll go down and talk to the sheriff in the morning."

"We could go now," Nannie said. "I'll go with you. I—"

"I'll go in the morning," Father said. "I'll talk to him and make sure he's investigating this. Whatever happened here, I don't think it was caused by sparks from the fireplace. Someone broke in to set this fire. This was arson."

As pleased as Nannie was to hear Father agree with her, she also felt frustration rise up. That was what she'd been trying to tell him! Still, now that Father was getting involved, she felt sure the sheriff would start taking this fire seriously.

CHAPTER FIVE

Father wouldn't let Nannie go with him to town in the morning.

"I could visit Molly," Nannie said, hopeful.

Father wasn't buying it. "You want to go and get in the middle of this thing," he said. "I told you, I'll handle it. I need you to take care of the chores, if I'm going to be gone all morning."

Nannie agreed to handle the barn chores, and then after breakfast, Father set off on Galway, the frisky gelding he preferred. Nannie hated being stuck at home. She hated being told to step aside and let the men handle things. Still, she did Father's chores as well as her own, and her heartbeat sped up when she heard hoofbeats coming up the road a few hours later. Father rode Galway, and the sheriff followed behind on his own roan horse. They rode right past the house and toward the burned-out store.

Nannie wanted to rush out and show the sheriff what she'd found and where she'd found it, but she remembered the sternness with which Father had told her he'd handle it. He would have stopped at the house to get her if he wanted her to talk to the sheriff. It took all of her self-control to focus on churning the butter, a task she hated but which needed to be done. She thought about hitching up the draft horse and heading out to the fields to plow, but she knew Father did not like her to work in the fields. It was indelicate and not something women did. Still, she was sorely tempted to risk her father's anger, just to give herself something to do. She thought she might jump out of her skin with anticipation when the sheriff finally climbed back onto his horse and started down the mountain again. Finally, after what seemed like hours, Father came to the house.

"What did he say?" Nannie asked before he'd even stepped through the front door.

"He agrees that it looks like arson," Father said. "He says it appears that someone did indeed break in and that kerosene was poured along the floor before a match was lit."

"It was arson?" Mother said weakly from the stove, where she was frying bread and slabs of ham for lunch.

"It was arson!" Nannie clapped her hands.

"It's not something to be excited about," Father said, his voice weary. "But yes, the sheriff agrees that this was no accident."

"I knew it wasn't," Nannie said. "I'm glad you finally got him to listen." She felt like a weight had come off her shoulders. The sheriff hadn't believed her, but he had believed Father, and now something could be done about it. "Is he going to arrest Everett?"

"He is going to talk to Everett," Father said. "As well as look into a few other clues."

"Other clues?"

Father nodded. "On the way up the hill, the sheriff spotted shattered glass. He thinks it might have been the jar that held the kerosene that was used to start the fire."

"There was glass by the road?" How had she missed that?

"There was," Father said. "Down by that first bend. I missed it too, Nan. I think the sun must have hit it at just the right angle so that the sheriff was able to see it. It was far enough off the road that it was hard to spot, especially in the shadows like it was. The thing is, the pieces smelled strongly of kerosene." He shook his head. "It looks like the kind of kerosene jar they sell at Radcliff's. You don't sell those jars in your shop, right?"

Nannie shook her head. Everyone brought their own jars for kerosene. "I just have—had—the big jugs. I refill the jars people bring me."

"That's what I told him," Father said.

Nannie tried to understand. It sounded like Father was saying someone had brought a bottle of kerosene up the hill, used it to set the blaze, and then dumped it by the side of the road.

"Why would someone carry kerosene up the hill when there was kerosene in the shop?" Nannie asked.

Father shrugged. "I can't say I understand why this person did anything he did," he said. "I don't pretend to understand the mind of the man who did this."

Nannie didn't understand it either.

"The sheriff will be investigating everything," Father said. "And I told him you would stay back and let him do his work." He gave her a significant look. "He believes it was arson, Nan. You won. Now let the man do his job."

"Of course," Nannie said. She would let the man do his job. Just as long as he actually did it.

"By the way, I ran into Ned Turner while I was in town," he continued. "He told me he was holding the supplies from your last shipment at the station for you."

"That's right," Nannie said.

"You'll need to go get them," Father said. "That was kind of him, but here." He walked to the cabinet and pulled down the wooden box where he kept their money. He handed her the coins she'd given to him the evening of the fire. This was money that was supposed to go to the bank. "I don't want to owe the Turner family anything."

CHAPTER SIX

Without the shop to run, Nannie didn't quite know what to do with herself the next day. She had gotten used to spending most of her time at the store and was out of the rhythm of helping around the house, but there was always plenty that needed to be done on a farm. Father went out to the fields, and Nannie did as she was asked, doing chores in the barn and helping Mother with housework.

It was nearing evening, and the stew was bubbling on the stove when a knock came at the door. Mother was elbow-deep in piecrust, so Nannie walked to the door and pulled it open.

"Frank?"

It was Frank Radcliff, holding a large basket covered by a dish towel. He wore his dress coat and hat. Nannie could see his horse was tied up by the road.

"I wanted to bring you this," he said, handing her the basket. "Just my way of saying I'm sorry for your troubles."

Inside the house, Lenore started talking excitedly to Mother, but Nannie couldn't hear what she was saying.

"I don't know what to say. Thank you." The basket was heavy, and when she pulled back the dish towel, she saw a loaf of bread and a wedge of cheese as well as jars of canned soup and peaches and beets. "This is wonderful," she said. "You packed this yourself?"

"Well, Mother sent along some things too," he said. "But it was my idea. We're all so sorry to hear what happened. I wish there was more we could do to help, but this is a start." He gave her a smile, and Nannie noticed a dimple in his left cheek. He wasn't bad looking, truthfully.

Behind her, Lenore had started to shriek. That wasn't unusual—she was quite sensitive—but Nannie hoped the sound wasn't disturbing Frank. Frank didn't seem to notice, though, or if he did, he was too polite to show it. She heard Mother trying to soothe Lenore behind her.

"This was nice," Nannie said. "Thank you."

Maybe it was just that her feelings were so raw, but suddenly the kindness that had grated on her before now suddenly felt like a balm to her soul. Frank *was* kind—this was more proof—and suddenly, Nannie wondered why she had ever thought kindness wasn't an appealing quality in a man.

"If there's any other way I can help, please let me know." Frank touched the brim of his hat and ducked his head, and then he turned and walked back down the wooden porch steps. Nannie watched him go, her mind spinning. As she watched him climb up into the saddle, she had an idea.

She set the heavy basket on the porch. "Frank!" she called. He turned back to her, his face shaded by the brim of his hat. She ran out the door and down the steps. "Frank, I was wondering…" She hesitated but then reminded herself he'd asked how he could help. Well, here was a way. "I have a load of supplies waiting for me at the station, from the latest shipment from Richmond. I was going to sell them at the shop, but, well…"

Frank nodded, encouraging her to go on.

"I was wondering—since I can't use them any longer, would you be interested in buying them from me?"

"Well, now." Frank rubbed his chin. "Of course, I'd love to help you out," he said slowly. "But we already have this week's shipment of supplies. I don't know that we could use more."

"I would sell them to you at a discount," Nannie said quickly. "You would be doing me a favor, and you would be getting supplies for your store at a good price." She wasn't begging. She was proposing a business deal. She watched as Frank considered her words.

"How steep a discount?" he finally asked.

Nannie named a price for the whole load and told him what was in it—flour, sugar, kerosene, lard, and various other supplies. The amount wouldn't cover the price she'd paid the supplier, but at least the whole load wouldn't sit and rot, and she'd get some money out of it.

"All right," Frank finally said. "If it will help you out, I suppose we could take those items off your hands for that price."

"Thank you." Nannie felt a weight lift from her shoulders. She'd get some money for the load, and that was better than losing it completely. "I appreciate it."

"Anything to help you out, Nannie." He gave her a shy smile.

Once again, she was grateful for his kindness. "You're doing me a great favor. I'll bring the load to you tomorrow," she promised.

"It's always a treat when I get to see you." Frank's smile widened. "I look forward to seeing you tomorrow." He ducked his head, and then he nudged his horse forward.

Nannie watched as he rode slowly down the hill. Something about him was different. Or maybe it was something about her. Whatever it was, Nannie suddenly found herself thinking about Frank differently. She watched until he vanished around the bend, and then she turned and headed back inside the house. As she stepped onto the porch, she heard Lenore still crying and Mother trying to soothe her. Nannie scooped up the basket, rushed inside, and hurried to see what had set her off.

"Lenore?" Mama held her youngest daughter, whose chest heaved with sobs. Tears streamed down Lenore's cheeks. "What is it?"

"It was him," Lenore said. "That was the man I saw the night of the fire."

"Frank?" Nannie blinked. "You couldn't have seen Frank."

"I did," Lenore said. "He had the same hat. I know it was him, Nannie."

Nannie tried to picture the view from Lenore's room. Could she really have seen a hat that clearly in the dark?

"It was him, Nannie. I know that hat. He was here that night. That was the man who set the fire."

∾ CHAPTER SEVEN ∾

The next morning, after the chores were done and Father was out in the fields, Nannie hitched Kildare to the buckboard. Once the wagon was secure and she'd climbed up into the driver's seat, she made the familiar journey down the mountain to town. It had rained the night before, and the mountain air was fresh and clean.

"'I will lift up mine eyes unto the hills, from whence cometh my help,'" Nannie recited softly. She never felt closer to the Lord than when she was out in these hills. She couldn't imagine wanting to live in a smoke-clogged city like Richmond. She hated to think what would happen to this quiet valley if the Turners were able to bring the railroad through here. The peace and serenity her family cherished would be gone forever.

Before she got to the outskirts of town, Nannie could hear the hiss of the coal-fired engine and smell the plumes of smoke. The morning train must have just come in. Nannie stopped her cart outside the station office and walked inside.

"—only an old abandoned building. Why would the town want to hang on to it?"

That sounded like Ned. She guessed he must be talking about the old schoolhouse, though it was hard to know for sure.

"It's not up to us." That was Everett. He said something more, but he lowered his voice, and she couldn't hear it. Just then, Ned looked up and saw her through the office window. He said something to Everett, and Everett stood up and shook his head. He walked out another door, away from the main part of the office.

Ned came out, smiling. "Good morning, Nannie," he said brightly. If she hadn't known better, she wouldn't have guessed that he'd just been arguing with his brother. "How are you holding up?"

"I'm doing all right," Nannie said. "The sun is shining, and the Lord is gracious."

"I'm glad to hear it," Ned said. "Have you come by for that shipment?" He indicated a pile of goods in the corner of the office—bags of flour and sugar, metal jugs containing oil, boxes of dried beans.

"I have. Thank you for holding it for me." She reached into the bag in her pocket and pulled out the last of the coins she'd earned in the shop.

"It wasn't a problem. I'm always happy to help, especially given what happened." He slipped the coins into his pocket. "Let me help you get these things loaded."

Ned hoisted the bags of flour and sugar, and Nannie grabbed the dried beans. They carried the goods out to the wagon, and together they had it loaded in just a few minutes. Nannie thanked Ned then drove the load down the road to Radcliff's. Hopefully, Frank would still take the whole shipment, even though it had been sitting for a few days and some of the items looked a bit worse for the wear.

She tied up Kildare, and then she walked inside and found Frank behind the counter. Radcliff's occupied a much larger building than Nannie's little store had. Shelves lined the walls, loaded with every kind of food she could think of—not just flour and beans and sugar but also salt pork and fresh vegetables and jars of oats and bran. There was a medicinal section where Frank sold quinine for stomach sickness and morphine tablets for toothaches and opium for pain relief. He sold seeds and scythes and animal feed, and rifles and ammunition and tobacco as well as fabric and ribbons and trimmings. Anything a person needed could be found at Radcliff's. Nannie had once dreamed that one day she might expand her store to rival it, but now she feared that wouldn't be possible.

Mrs. Wilde from out by Rocky Ridge Road was going through the bolts of calico, and she looked up and waved at Nannie as she walked in. Nannie also saw Jimmy Radcliff, Frank's older brother, explaining the benefits of different soap powders to Frederick Banner, who ran the print shop.

"Good morning, Nannie." Frank smiled at her from behind the counter. Nannie tried to return the expression, but the warm feelings that she had felt for Frank yesterday had soured after Lenore's revelation. Had it truly been Frank that Lenore had seen from her bedroom window? The bowler hat with the blue grosgrain ribbon *was* distinctive. It had been dark, but that didn't mean Lenore was mistaken. Once the thought was planted in her mind, Nannie couldn't help wondering.

"Hello, Frank. I have that shipment of goods out in the wagon."

"Great. Let me help you bring it in."

Frank carried in the heavy items Ned had just put into the wagon. As he brought in the second bag of beans, Nannie saw the bandage on his wrist once more.

"How is your arm?" she asked, gesturing at the bandage. "Is it healing all right?"

"What?" Frank set the bag of dried beans on the counter, looked down at his arm, and then quickly pulled the edge of his sleeve over the bandage. "Oh, yes. Much better." Then he turned and headed out to bring in another load. Nannie puzzled over this strange reaction for a moment, but then she hurried outside to carry in more of the bags.

When everything was inside, Frank surveyed the items and named the price again. It was far less than they were worth, but Nannie didn't see what choice she had. Frank went behind the counter, moved aside the accounts book and his hat, and began to count out the coins slowly. The Radcliffs allowed customers to purchase items on credit, and the ledger book was where they kept a record of who had bought what items on credit and how much they needed to pay. So many farmers—her family included—scraped by on credit through the lean months until they could pay the full amount back after harvest. Nannie was sure her father's name was in the book more times than he liked.

While Frank double-checked his math, Nannie let her eyes drift to the section of shelving where the glass jars of kerosene were sold. Had the one that lay shattered on Rocky Ridge Road come from Radcliff's?

"Here you go, Nannie." Frank held out the coins, and she took them and put them in her cloth bag.

"That's a nice hat you've got there," Nannie said, gesturing toward the bowler. "Is that new?"

"I got it on a trip to visit family in Raleigh a few weeks back," Frank said. "My cousin Mabel tells me ribbons like this are all the rage in the big city, and she insisted I purchase one, but I don't know. It doesn't seem to have caught on around here yet."

"It's very nice. And very distinctive," Nannie said.

"I suppose it is." He gave her a shy smile. "Thank you."

Nannie couldn't help herself. She knew she should go, and leave this to the authorities as Father had said, but since she was here, she had to ask.

"It's funny, because Lenore is certain she saw someone wearing a hat just like this ride past the house Monday night," she said. "But you wouldn't have been riding past our house that night, would you?"

"What?" Frank's eyes widened. "N-no. Absolutely not." He shook his head.

"Huh." She didn't believe him. He protested far too much for someone who hadn't been there. He had ridden out to Rocky Ridge, and he was shocked that he'd been found out. She was sure of it.

"Are you sure? Lenore seemed pretty certain. She recognized your hat when you came by yesterday."

"I'm sure." He said it with a little more confidence this time. "Why would I be out by your place at night? That doesn't make any sense."

He was lying. She hadn't known what to think about Lenore's claims before, but hearing how strongly he denied what she knew to be true made her more suspicious.

"Now, is there anything else you need?" Frank's smile was too wide, his eyes darting off to the side. "If not, I need to go help Mrs. Wilde."

"Go ahead," Nannie said. "And thank you."

Frank nodded and raced to the other side of the store. *He can't get away fast enough*, Nannie thought as she placed the little bag back in her pocket and turned to go.

Nannie didn't want to deal with the sheriff and face his derision again, but she couldn't just ignore the fact that there was a new lead for him to investigate. Still, she was pretty sure she knew how she was going to be received. She decided to make one stop before she went to the sheriff. Molly would help her think through this and let her know if she was being ridiculous.

She climbed into the wagon and steered it down Third Street. She tied Kildare to the hitching post in front of the house and then walked up the porch steps. The Campbell house truly was a work of art, with its gingerbread trim and its dentils and moldings on every surface. It was painted in shades of green and red and brown and cream, and it was by far the prettiest—and largest—house in town. She knocked on the door, and a minute later it was pulled open.

Elsa, the Campbells' stoic but dependable maid, stood in the doorway.

"Miss Campbell is not receiving visitors at the moment." Elsa wore a black dress covered by a white apron, and her hair was arranged in a severe bun. "But if you'll leave your card—"

"I'm here!" Molly came bounding down the hallway behind Elsa. She wore a morning dress of sprigged muslin, and her long hair was loose around her shoulders. "It's just Nannie, Elsa. She can come in."

"You are not dressed for visitors, miss," Elsa said archly, but Molly waved aside the maid's words. Elsa gave both of them a disapproving look before retreating.

"Come in," Molly said, pulling on Nannie's hand. She led Nannie into the parlor, which was papered in a dark floral print and hung with velvet curtains. "I need to know what's happened. Has the sheriff arrested Everett yet?" Molly sat down on a crewel-work settee and indicated Nannie should sit on another.

"Not that I know of," Nannie said. "But I'm starting to wonder if there might be another possibility for what happened."

Molly cocked her head.

"Last night, Frank Radcliff came out to our place with a basket of food."

"See?" Molly looked triumphant. "He wants to court you, Nannie. Why not give him a chance?"

"Hang on. Listen, before you go marrying me off."

"I'm just saying—"

"Molly, wait. Listen to this. Lenore started screaming when she saw him. She'd told me earlier that she saw a man in a bowler hat outside the house the night of the fire."

"Okay. But so many men wear bowler hats—"

"But Frank's hat is different, with that blue ribbon."

"I do remember it," Molly said slowly, "because it looks like the way men are wearing their hats in Richmond, and I was surprised to see it on Frank. But that doesn't mean—"

"Lenore knew it was the same hat. She was certain it was Frank she saw."

Molly pressed her lips together. She thought for a moment and then said, "It would have been dark, wouldn't it? How can she be sure?"

Nannie could see Molly had the same doubts she herself had wrestled with at first. She needed to share the rest of what she knew.

"Do you remember how, the day after the fire, Frank had a bandage on his wrist?"

Molly's brow wrinkled. "That's right. He said he cut it on a barrel."

"I thought it sounded strange at the time, and now I know why."

"Are you thinking he might have hurt himself when he broke in to set the fire?"

"Yes," Nannie said, nodding. "Plus, there was that broken kerosene bottle the sheriff found by the road out near our place."

"What?" Molly's eyes widened, and Nannie realized she hadn't yet filled her friend in on what the sheriff had said. She told Molly the story and then added, "Radcliff's sells the kind of kerosene bottle the sheriff found."

Molly was quiet for a moment, and then she shook her head.

"What?" Nannie asked.

"I don't want to believe it," Molly said. "I can't believe it. But I just realized he's got a motive too."

"He does?"

Molly nodded. "The Radcliffs have been losing customers ever since you opened your shop."

"They have?" Nannie blinked in surprise. "I can't imagine my little shop has had much of an impact on the Radcliffs' store."

"It has though. Paul Radcliff came to my father about a loan a few weeks ago, saying business has been dropping since your shop opened." She shook her head. "Oh, don't look at me like that, Nan. It's not my fault if my father speaks freely because he assumes I don't understand what they're talking about. What matters is that I know that Radcliff's has been losing sales since you became their competition. Which means Frank Radcliff has good reason to want your shop closed down. Which means…" Her eyes widened. "Oh Nannie, do you think that's why he's been so attentive to you? Because he's hoping you'll marry him and close your store?"

Nannie tried not to let the words sting.

"I don't mean to imply that he couldn't like you for you, of course," Molly added quickly. "It's just that I can see an ulterior motive."

"Only a few days ago you were suggesting that my marrying him would be an ideal outcome," Nannie said.

"But that was before I knew he might be the one who set fire to your store," Molly said. "To get rid of the competition. Maybe he got tired of waiting for you to say yes to him and went this route instead to run you out of business."

"I hate to admit it," Nannie said. "But I do think it's a possibility. And when I asked Frank if he'd been out near our place that night, he denied it so forcefully that it made me sure he was lying."

"Oh my." Molly sighed. "Have you told the sheriff?"

"No," Nannie said. "I wanted to talk to you first, to see whether you thought I was making wrong assumptions."

"No, I don't think you are," Molly said. "I think you should go over there right now and tell the sheriff to investigate Frank Radcliff."

"Thank you." Nannie started to push herself up, but then she noticed that Molly had a strange expression on her face.

"What is it?" Nannie asked.

"I was just thinking." Molly smiled slyly. "What if it was Frank who set the fire? That would mean Everett didn't do it, right?"

"I guess." Nannie realized what this meant. She felt terrible for dragging his name through the mud if he wasn't the one responsible. "But what's that look for?"

"If Everett didn't set that fire, then maybe you don't have to hate him after all." Molly seemed pleased as punch with this possibility. "Maybe you could even get to know him better."

Nannie laughed. "Don't count on it. Even if he didn't set that fire, he's still a Turner."

"You would make the handsomest couple. And he's rich, to boot. I bet if you gave him half a chance, you would fall right in love with Everett Turner."

Nannie laughed. "I could never fall in love with Everett Turner."

～ Chapter Eight ～

The same men were sitting in the same places when Nannie walked into the town hall again. The one at the front desk looked up at her languidly.

"I'm here to see Sheriff Bush," she announced.

"He's out," said the one behind the counter.

"I'll wait."

The man pointed to a wooden chair by the door, and Nannie sat down and arranged her skirt carefully. The men turned to their work. Nannie got the sense they weren't usually this quiet, but they weren't talking in her presence. The one at the back desk—who had a few long strands of hair combed across his otherwise bald head— kept sneaking glances at her. She wasn't sure how long she sat there, but it felt like an eternity before the door opened and the sheriff stepped in. He nodded at Nannie, and then he started across the room toward his office.

"Miss Starkey is here to see you," the first man said.

"I see that," Sheriff Bush said. Nannie tried to ignore the weariness in his voice. "Come on back, Miss Starkey."

She ignored the prying eyes of the men as she made her way across the room and into the office.

"If you're here to learn more about my investigation," he started, "I told your father—"

"That's not why I'm here," Nannie said. "I need to let you know what I've learned." She told him about Lenore's conviction that she'd seen Frank on the road the night of the fire.

"Miss Starkey, your sister is…seven years old?"

"Eight," Nannie said.

"Please don't take this the wrong way, Miss Starkey, but we can't seriously consider a man a suspect because of something a little girl thinks she saw in the dark."

"Lenore is very observant." She tried not to let his words sting.

"Your sister is very sweet." He leaned back in his wooden chair, which groaned under him. "But with her challenges…" He gestured absently. "You must see why I have to take this testimony with a grain of salt."

"There's nothing wrong with her mind, Sheriff." The words came out a little stronger than she intended. "Her body may not always work as yours or mine does, but she is as sharp as they come, and if she says she saw someone wearing Frank's hat, I believe her. Besides, Frank sells bottles of kerosene at Radcliff's—"

"Which anyone in town could have bought, seeing as how they sell them to anyone."

"And he has a good motive to want my store to close. You need to look into Frank Radcliff."

"Miss Starkey, a few days ago, you were in here convinced that Everett Turner had set the fire. Now you're sure it's Frank Radcliff. Who will it be tomorrow? Should I wait while you drag the name of every upstanding man in this town through the mud?"

She couldn't believe it. He was dismissing her, just like that. "I'm asking you to look into a viable suspect, based on clues and eyewitness testimony."

Sheriff Bush smiled, but the smile didn't reach his eyes. "Well, I thank you for your advice on how to do my job. Now, if you'll excuse me, I have work to get to."

She left the office deflated. He hadn't taken her seriously, even when she had solid clues to present. He had dismissed her ideas, and he had insulted Lenore. She rushed out of the building and almost walked right into a man coming up the steps.

"Excuse me," she said quickly, stepping back, but the heel of her boot caught, and she felt herself start to lose her balance. A strong arm shot out and grabbed her, steadying her.

"I'm so sorry, Nannie." Everett. The man who had nearly knocked her over was Everett Turner. "Are you okay? I didn't mean to startle you."

"I'm fine," she said, wrenching her arm from his grasp. "I just didn't expect to see anyone there."

"It's my fault. I was in such a rush I wasn't paying as much attention as I should have," Everett said. "I was coming to find you, actually."

"Me?" Why was Everett looking for her at the sheriff's office? And why was the sight of those warm brown eyes making her so unsettled?

"That's your wagon, isn't it?" He gestured to where Kildare was hitched up in front of the town hall.

"Yes," she said warily.

"I thought it was. I saw it outside the office earlier when you met with Ned. And when I saw it here, I noticed that one of the spokes on your wheel was cracked. I figured you must be inside, so I came to tell you."

"What?" What was he talking about?

He gestured for her to follow him, and they walked down the steps and into the street. He went to the buckboard, leaned over, and pointed at one of the spokes on the wagon's left front wheel. "See here?" he said.

He was right. The wooden spoke was cracked right down the middle. When had this happened? The wheel was fine earlier.

"If you drive up the hill on this, the whole wheel could break," Everett said. "And you'd be stranded."

He was right. She should take it to the wheelwright's, over by the train station. But it would cost all the coins she'd just gotten from Frank, and more, to get this fixed.

"I don't understand," she said. "How could this have happened? It wasn't like this earlier." Had someone tampered with her wagon while she was at the train station or in talking to the sheriff?

"I couldn't say what led to it," Everett said. "But you shouldn't drive on it. You don't want to break down halfway up that hill."

"I'll have to drive on it," she said. She didn't see another option. Once she got the wagon home, Father would know what to do. "I can't just leave it here."

"I can do a temporary fix," Everett said. "If you come with me to the shop, I can fit a new spoke in there for you."

She narrowed her eyes. "You can?"

"Sure. It won't be pretty, but I could fix it enough to get you home safely on that wheel. It should be all right until you can go to the wheelwright."

She didn't want to go to the shop with Everett. But she wasn't sure what else to do. He was right—if the wheel broke and she got stuck halfway up the hill, she'd be in big trouble. But something didn't add up, and before she went with him, she had to ask.

"How did you happen to notice that broken spoke?"

Everett hesitated. He pressed his lips together, waiting just a moment too long. "I was walking past, and I noticed it," he finally said.

That was completely implausible. She knew right away that this wasn't the truth. The crack was wide, but it was also hidden on the top of the spoke, out of the line of sight of someone simply walking past. He would have had to have gotten quite close to see it. Had he been poking around her wagon? Or was there some other explanation?

"You know, I think I'll just take my chances getting home," she said, starting for the wagon.

"Wait. Please. Nannie, you can't." Everett stepped toward her. "You'll get stuck. It's not safe. Let me help you." He gazed directly into her eyes.

Something in her wanted to believe him. The way he looked at her, it was almost as if he saw into her soul, and something inside of her recognized the truth of his words. But she also couldn't ignore the fact that what he said didn't make sense. He couldn't have seen the crack if he'd been simply walking past. Not to mention, he was still a prime suspect for the arson.

"You don't think I had something to do with it, do you?" Everett's eyes widened. "Nannie, I promise you, I did not touch your wagon. You can't seriously believe I would do this."

"I don't know what to believe," she said truthfully. She gazed up at him. Molly was right—he really was a very nice-looking man. Those high cheekbones, those warm brown eyes, those lips…

Beneath the handsome face, she also saw the traces of the boy she'd once known. The boy she'd once trusted and cared for. Had he truly changed so much over the years? She'd been sure the answer was yes at first. Now... Now, she wasn't so sure.

"I promise you, Nannie, all I want to do is help you," he said. Something in her lurched, longing to believe him.

"Why?" she asked.

"Do I truly need a reason to help an old friend?" he asked.

Yes. "I may be an old friend, but I also stand between you and that railroad spur your father wants so badly."

"Nannie." He took a step closer. "Please, just trust me."

She wanted to. With everything in her, she wanted to. But she didn't know him anymore. His years away had changed him, surely. The reality of what he stood to lose if his father wasn't successful was too big to ignore. She didn't know what to say. She finally made herself look away.

Everett must have taken her silence for acquiescence.

"Let's go get this wheel fixed up," he said. She hadn't agreed to go with him, but he didn't seem to care. He untied the reins and talked softly to the horse, who stepped back from the hitching post and followed Everett toward the road. Nannie didn't know what else to do, so she hurried to catch up. She walked beside Everett as he led her horse and wagon down the center of the main road. She saw several people turn to watch the odd little parade.

"The sheriff came and talked to me," Everett said as they walked. "About the fire."

"Did he?" Nannie kept her voice level, hoping she wouldn't reveal anything.

"He seemed to think I had a nefarious reason for being out by your place that night." Everett kept his eyes facing forward, his steps unhurried as he led the horse and wagon through town.

"What did you tell him?" Nannie asked.

"I told him the truth. That I was glad I was there to alert you all, but that I had nothing to do with starting it."

He said it so simply, so earnestly. It hit her differently than Frank's denial. She wanted to believe him, but she didn't know if she could.

"So what *were* you doing out by our place?" she asked.

Everett didn't answer. A muscle in his jaw worked.

"You must have had a reason," Nannie said. "You didn't just happen to be going past."

Everett didn't answer for another minute, and then he said, "This town has changed. It's strange to be back and see how much it's grown since I left."

Nannie was stunned. Was he going to ignore her question? "Everett, why were you there the night of the fire?" she demanded.

He continued as if he hadn't heard her.

"This place used to feel like a small town. I knew everyone and everything they did. Now, there are so many new people."

"That's got a lot to do with the railroad bringing more people to the area," Nannie said. "But that doesn't answer my question."

"No," he admitted. "It doesn't." He sighed. "The truth is, it's not something I want to talk about. But still, I'm asking you to trust me, Nannie. I had nothing to do with starting the fire. I promise you that."

Nannie's stomach sank. The only conclusion she could come to was that if he hadn't been out on Rocky Ridge Road to set the fire, there was only one other place he could have been heading. His reticence to admit what he was doing there only made her more certain she was right. And as much as she didn't want to believe he'd set the fire, the idea that he'd been out there to visit Hanson's made her feel unexpectedly disappointed.

She was right in thinking he'd changed.

They walked in silence. As they neared the rail yard, she heard the clang of metal striking metal, and the smell of grease and coal soot hung in the air. Here was where the train cars were repaired and adjustments were made when needed. The train station—with its bustling crowds and its engines belching steam—was just down the tracks. The Turners' office was at the station, but Everett walked into the rail yard as if he owned it.

They walked through a small wooden building, more a shack lined with tools than anything else, and into the open yard, which was threaded with train tracks. Several train cars—passenger cars, cargo cars, even one that looked like it had once carried coal—were in various states of disrepair on the tracks. A few men were gathered around one of the passenger cars, using a claw bar to try to dislodge something stuck in the underside. Nannie recognized Earl Miller, who leered at her as she followed Everett.

The yard was loud and ugly and smelled terrible, and if Everett's father got his way, more of these metal beasts would be slicing right through the Starkey land soon.

"There are metal rods over here," Everett said. He opened a cabinet and rooted through a collection of bars of various sizes. After a few moments of searching, he pulled out three and then gestured for her to follow him. He led her back through the small toolshed, where he grabbed a pair of pliers and what looked like a hammer but with a bigger, square metal head. He set the tools down, took off his hat and coat and set them in the wagon, and rolled up his sleeves. She tried not to notice his strong forearms and wide shoulders.

"You're a lawyer," Nannie said as he began to tap at the broken piece of wood with the hammer. "How do you know how to repair a wagon wheel?"

"I'm not really fixing it," Everett said as he worked. "This is more of a short-term solution. But don't forget, I grew up around trains. Ned and I spent hours roaming around this place when we were kids. You pick things up." He knocked at the spoke one more time, harder, and it broke from the rim with a splintering crack.

"I remember you and Ned roaming all over town, not just around here." Nannie smiled. "You always seemed to be around and looking for something to do whenever I came into town."

"Yes, well." He held up the broken spoke and handed it to her. What was she supposed to do with it? "After Mother passed away, we didn't have a lot of supervision. Dad was busy working, and Ned and I were left to our own devices most of the time, at least until we were old enough to help in the office."

Nannie had forgotten his mother had passed when he and Ned were children. She had been taken when yellow fever swept through the area.

"I'm sorry," she said.

"For what?" Everett picked up one of the metal rods, sizing it up.

"For your mother. I'd forgotten."

"Oh. Thanks. It was a long time ago."

Nannie was sure he still missed her, even if he didn't show it. If anything happened to her mother, Nannie would never get over it. And then she realized something. "I was always jealous of how you were free to do what you wanted when we were young. You could spend hours fishing by the creek, but I couldn't spend the day just having fun. I guess I never understood why you could roam around town like you did."

"Benign neglect does have its benefits." Everett shrugged. "But really, Dad did his best. It's just that he was so busy trying to build the station, and he wasn't prepared to raise two boys on his own. And he was dealing with grief. He never seemed to recover, honestly. It changed him. That was when he started dreaming about adding the Lynchburg spur, and he also wanted one for Charlottesville." He set the iron rod aside and picked up another, holding it near the wheel to see if it would fit. It was about as big around as her finger and looked to be about the same length as the broken spoke. "I can see now why he threw himself into his work, though at the time, all I knew was that it felt like I'd lost my father as well as my mother."

"I'm so sorry." Once again, she saw how little she'd understood about Everett's life when they were young. All she'd seen was a willing playmate who was there whenever she made it to town.

Instead of answering, he began to fit the metal piece into the hole left by the broken spoke.

"The thing is," he finally said, "I didn't just happen to be around when you came to town."

"What?"

"You said I always seemed to be around when you came to town. But it wasn't by happenstance. I waited around, hoping you'd show up."

"You did?"

"I did." Everett pushed against the wooden wheel with the rod until he was able to snap it into the hub.

"You had all the town kids to play with though."

"But you were always my favorite. You weren't prissy, like the other girls. You were always ready to catch tadpoles or race me to the corner. You were different. I think I was probably a little bit in love with you, if I'm being honest."

Nannie was so shocked she didn't know what to say. But Everett said briskly, "There you go. That should hold, at least until you can get to the wheelwright." He tapped the wheel with his palm.

"Thank you," Nannie stammered. "I appreciate it."

"It's the least I can do." Everett looked like he was going to say more, but then he smiled, picked up his tools, his hat, and his coat, and walked back inside. Nannie climbed into the wagon, puzzling over what had just happened and what it all meant.

✑ Chapter Nine ✑

Saturday morning dawned clear and warm, and though it was still February, Nannie began to hope that spring might be on the way. She climbed out of bed and got dressed and then helped Father with the chores as the rising sun brightened the sky. She had lain awake last night, replaying the conversation with Everett in her mind, trying to make sense of it.

What had he meant when he'd said helping her was the least he could do? Was he admitting he had something to pay her back for—the fire?—after all? But he'd promised her he hadn't set the fire, and something inside her said to believe him.

And had he really said he used to be in love with her? Why couldn't she stop thinking about that moment, about the way he'd looked at her when he said the words? She felt a flutter in her belly every time.

She needed to stop thinking about him. She decided on a task for the day, and after she helped Mother clean up the kitchen, she put on her oldest dress, pulled on her heaviest boots, grabbed a pair of work gloves from the shed, wheeled out the wheelbarrow, and headed out across the yard toward the remains of the store. The morning sun cast the burnt chimney in a warm glow, and it almost looked cheerful.

Once she reached the site, she surveyed the mess, uncertain where to begin. Finally, she just decided to start with what was right in front of her. She picked up a charred piece of timber that looked like it used to be part of the floor. Her hands and dress were immediately covered in soot, but she didn't care. She dragged the timber to the edge of the clearing and dropped it. The site needed to be cleaned up if she was going to rebuild, and she was tired of sitting around waiting for something to happen.

After she dropped the piece of wood, she went back to the charred remains and picked up the next piece of timber and dragged it to the edge of the clearing. It wasn't nearly as heavy as it should have been, since so much had been burned away. Slowly, one timber at a time, she dragged the broken remains of the building to the pile. It would take her days to get the space cleared, she could see that now.

If only there was someone to help her—but if there had been someone all these years, they wouldn't be in the situation they were in. If Nannie had brothers... But it didn't do any good wishing. Father had to be in the fields, and if he wouldn't let her help there, she would focus on this herself. She would just have to keep at it until the land was clear so they could rebuild. Well, they could rebuild as soon as they knew who had set the fire. That person would have to reimburse them for their loss.

An hour later, she had made dozens of trips carrying charred wood to the pile, and she still had hundreds more to go. She stopped and straightened up and brushed her forearm across her face. The air was cold, but she was working up a sweat. She went back again, this time loading a pile of debris into the wheelbarrow. Once it was full, she wheeled it around the woodpile she'd made and moved a little farther into the woods before she dumped the charred wood and broken glass. But as the debris tumbled out of the wheelbarrow, something in the underbrush caught her eye. What was that? There was something dark lying at the base of a pine tree. Something long, and it looked like metal. When she got closer, she bent over and gasped.

She knew what it was. She'd seen something just like it yesterday, and she knew exactly what it meant.

"You're saying that you went to town and told Sheriff Bush to look into Frank Radcliff yesterday, but now you want me to go down there and tell him it was Everett Turner after all?"

Father's voice was weary.

"I thought it was Frank before I found this," Nannie said, gesturing at the railroad claw bar on the workbench in the barn. The light from the dying day cast beams of weak sunlight through the cracks between the boards. Kildare and Galway pushed against the doors of their stalls, eager for dinner, but Nannie and Father stood just inside the barn, where Nannie had stopped him as soon as he came in from the fields.

"This would make exactly the kind of marks that we found on the door of the shop, right?" Nannie gestured at the piece of metal, about four feet long and narrow all the way down except for a curved claw at the end. There were a few dark brown spots on the handle, which Nannie thought might be blood.

"It does look like it could have been the tool used to pry open the door," Father said reluctantly. "It's usually used for pulling up railroad spikes, and yes, it would probably leave the kind of marks we found."

"And I saw one just like it down at the rail yard yesterday," Nannie said. "When Everett helped me with the wagon wheel. He told me he and Ned practically grew up there. He knows how to use the tools. And who else would have access to one of these?" The facts all lined up.

"I don't know," Father said with a sigh. "I suppose anyone who works at the rail yard, or anyone who wandered inside. Judging by the fact that you went in, I'm guessing the security isn't that tight. Is there any reason you think it has to be Everett?"

"Who else would it have been?" Nannie insisted. The words tore through a tender place inside her as they came out. She had believed him, she realized now. Despite knowing that she shouldn't trust him, somewhere deep inside, she had believed Everett when he'd promised her he had nothing to do with the fire, and it hurt to admit that she had been taken in. That she'd trusted him, when he was so clearly undeserving of it. She'd fallen for his good looks and his smooth talk. He'd manipulated her—she saw that now so clearly. "Who else with any connection to the rail yard would want to burn down my shop?"

Father didn't say anything for a moment. He shifted his weight from one foot to the other.

"What is it?" There was something he wasn't saying.

"I'll take this to the sheriff," he finally said. "And I'll tell him where you found it. And then I'll let him do his own investigation into how it got there."

"But you'll tell him about how Everett knows his way around the rail yard, right?" Nannie asked.

Father sighed. "I will let the sheriff do his own investigation."

in Burnt Chimney, Virginia

"You don't think it was Everett, do you?" Nannie couldn't understand it. Sure, she had thought Frank was the guilty party yesterday, but they didn't sell claw bars at Radcliff's. "Even though he has the most to gain if we lose this land, you don't think he did it, do you?"

"I don't know," Father said. "Why don't we wait and see what the sheriff has to say?"

Nannie was so sick of waiting to hear what the sheriff had to say. He didn't seem to have any new leads or be making any progress.

"The truth will come out," Father said. "I believe that our God is just, and I trust that He will bring the truth to light. Do you trust Him as well?"

"Yes," Nannie said. She did. She knew God was in control of all things. "But God sure doesn't seem to be in any sort of hurry, does He?"

"It's all in His hands," Father said. "Try to trust."

"I'll do my best," Nannie said.

She wished she had the deep, unshakeable faith Father had. Nannie had seen God do incredible things, and she knew Father was right. But that didn't make it any easier to wait and let the sheriff do all the investigating.

She would trust God.

But that didn't mean she would give up trying to solve the mystery.

∽ Chapter Ten ∾

Saturday night after supper, Nannie helped Father haul water from the well to the stove and then into the old metal tub. Twenty minutes later, a week's worth of grime and grit washed away as she lowered herself into the tub. Lenore and Mother had bathed before her, and the water smelled sweet with the perfumed soap powder Mother bought for Lenore's delicate skin. Nannie used a washcloth to rub the soap up and down her arms, luxuriating in the warm water for a few minutes before she climbed out and wrapped herself in a thin cotton towel. She pulled her nightclothes on quickly, bracing herself against the chill of the evening air, and then called to Father to let him know the bath was free. Tomorrow morning was church, and they would all show up looking clean and smelling fresh.

Father had dutifully ridden into town that afternoon, taking the claw bar with him, and when he returned a few hours later, he wouldn't say much about the trip except that the sheriff now had the tool and would look into it. Nannie tried to let that be enough, tried to rest in the knowledge that God would bring the truth to light. Still, thoughts swirled in her head for much of the night, and she had trouble sleeping.

Sunday morning dawned clear and bright, and Mother sang as she boiled oatmeal and fried bacon. After the chores were done and the breakfast dishes put away, they all climbed into the carriage.

Mother held the bowl of potatoes she'd prepared for the covered dinner that would be held after the service. Father sat in the driver's seat, Mother beside him, while Lenore and Nannie sat in the second row of leather-covered seats. Father told Galway to go, and the horse started walking. They only used the carriage when Mother and Lenore went into town, and it was much more comfortable than the wagon or riding horseback. The buckboard was out of commission until they could get it repaired, so Nannie was glad they had the carriage. She did her best to listen as Lenore chattered on about Billy Perkins, who had promised to give her a boiled sweet after the service.

They rolled up to the church, a white clapboard building with a tall white steeple, just before the service started, and Nannie followed her parents to their usual pew. Molly was seated with her own parents in their pew, the one with her family's name engraved on it. A purple wide-brimmed hat trimmed in tulle and feathers was perched on her head, and her mother wore a similar hat in powder blue. As the first song started, with elderly Phyllis Himmelman wheezing out the tune on the pump organ, Nannie saw that the Turners were also seated in their family's pew.

She forced herself to keep her eyes trained away from Everett's broad shoulders. His coat was just tight enough to reveal the muscles in his shoulders, and his dark hair was perfectly combed. He was half a head taller than Ned, who stood next to him with his sandy hair and thicker frame, his very pregnant wife and two children beside him. The Radcliffs sat opposite the Starkeys in the pews that were open to all. Nannie felt Frank trying to catch her eye at a few points during the service, but she kept her gaze averted. She spent much of the service looking at the words in the Bible in her lap, where it was safe to let her gaze rest.

After the service ended, Molly hurried to Nannie and linked arms with her. "So?" Molly said. "What happened with the sheriff?"

"Let's wait until we get outside," Nannie said, and Molly nodded, understanding. Together they greeted Pastor Mullins in the narthex before stepping out into the sunshine. They walked down the steps and into the shade of a towering oak, whose limbs were studded with fresh green buds.

"I told the sheriff about Frank," Nannie said once she was sure they were out of earshot. People filed out of the church in a steady stream, eager for sunlight and fresh air after the somber sermon. "But listen to this. You'll never guess what I found in the woods yesterday."

Nannie told Molly about the railroad claw bar and about Father's trip to town to tell the sheriff about the new development.

"And you think that proves it was Everett…why?" Molly asked.

Nannie sighed. She realized she hadn't told Molly about what had happened with him. She related how Everett had discovered her broken wheel and fixed it at the rail yard.

"So…you're suggesting Everett broke the spoke of your wheel and then fixed it?" Molly asked, blinking. "And that this means he was responsible for the fire?"

"The claw bar is what makes me sure he set the fire," Nannie said. "I was at the rail yard, where there were lots of claw bars. He had access."

"And what about the fact that he fixed your wheel?" Molly said. "Why would he do that if he has it out for you?"

"He obviously broke the wheel to begin with," Nannie said. "So he could swoop in and look like a hero. It's like what happened when he set the fire."

Molly didn't say anything. She was watching the door of the church, where the Turner family had just stepped out. Everett looked good in his dark blue suit, and Nannie's heartbeat sped up when she saw him standing there in the sunlight. He scanned the churchyard and smiled when he saw Nannie and Molly. He nodded, but just then Mr. Taylor, the farrier, clapped his hand on Everett's back, and Everett turned toward him.

"He kept looking at you during the service," Molly said.

"What? No he didn't."

"Yes, he did."

"I was behind him."

"He kept looking back."

"You couldn't have possibly seen that from where you were."

"I could, and I did." Molly gave her a sly smile. "I think he's smitten."

"I think you're out of your mind," Nannie said. "Everett is not interested in me. Never mind the fact that I just told you I've got him at the top of the suspect list again."

Most of the congregation was outside the building now. A swarm of children ran around the lawn that led down to the gravestones. Lenore hobbled behind them, doing her best to keep up. Nannie saw Mother talking with some of the other ladies, while Father was—

Oh. Father was deep in conversation with Warren Campbell, Molly's father. What were they talking about so intensely?

"I have to admit, I don't see how finding that claw bar makes him the prime suspect," Molly said. "Lots of people have access to tools like that."

"Like who? Frank doesn't. They don't sell them at the general store." Frank and his father were talking to the cooper at the side of the church.

"What about Earl Miller, for instance?" Molly glanced toward the corner of the churchyard. Earl stood awkwardly beside his wife, Ludmilla, who was talking animatedly with Minnie Ryder, the wife of another rail worker. Earl looked uncomfortable in his pressed pants and starched shirt, and he seemed like he was ready to bolt any minute.

"Earl?" She hadn't thought about Earl.

"Doesn't he work down at the rail yard?" Molly asked.

"Yes, I guess he does," Nannie said. She'd seen him there. And he'd been using a claw bar, actually. Out of the corner of her eye, she saw Everett shake Mr. Taylor's hand and then walk toward the lawn.

"He hasn't exactly been quiet about the fact that he thinks a woman shouldn't run a store," Molly said. "Maybe it was him."

"Maybe." Now that Molly mentioned it, Nannie wasn't sure how she hadn't thought of Earl before this. Earl was adamant that a woman's place was in the home and that Nannie was usurping the natural order of things by trying to run a business. He also had access to a claw bar. Could he have felt so strongly about it that he took matters into his own hands? "You know, it is a possibility," she said, nodding.

"Nannie?"

Both Nannie and Molly turned to see that Frank Radcliff had walked up beside them.

"I was wondering if you might want to take a stroll around the block," Frank said, holding out his arm. His sleeve rode up, and Nannie saw his bandage peeking out once again.

She froze.

The bandage on his arm. It had been there since the night of the fire. And she'd seen dark spots on the claw bar. Had Frank hurt himself using the claw bar to break into the store?

"I—"

The last thing she wanted to do was go for a walk with Frank, especially now. She still had too many questions about what he was doing on Rocky Ridge Road that night.

"I'm...I'm afraid I can't," she stammered.

"You can't?" Frank blinked. "Why not?"

"I have to go...do something," Nannie said, and hated herself the moment the words came out. Couldn't she have come up with something better than that?

"She's terribly busy," Molly said. "So much to do. I'm sure you understand." She pulled on Nannie's arm, rescuing her from the uncomfortable moment. "So many people she has to talk to. Let's go." Nannie took a step just as Frank said, "Like who?"

"Me, I'm afraid."

They all turned, and Nannie sucked in a breath when she saw Everett Turner standing there. "Nannie, I need to speak with you," he said.

Nannie looked from Everett to Frank and back again. Both of them were suspects on her list. Either could have been responsible for the fire. Both of them had lied to her. Her mind said she shouldn't trust either one of them. And yet, she'd felt nothing but distaste about a walk with Frank, while the thought of walking with Everett made her stomach flutter. Her mind didn't believe she could trust him. But her heart wasn't sure it cared.

Everett didn't wait for her to answer. He placed his hand on her arm and tugged gently. Molly immediately let go, and Nannie found she was walking away with Everett, leaving Frank and Molly behind.

"That was quite bold," Nannie said. She had to skip a bit to keep up with him. "What made you think I wanted to come with you?"

Everett smirked. "Oh, I'm sorry. Did you want to go back and take a walk with Frank Radcliff?"

She let out a sigh. "No. But that doesn't mean I wanted to walk with you either."

"And yet here you are," Everett said, the smug smile still on his face.

"I wouldn't smile about being the lesser of two evils," Nannie said.

"That's not why I'm smiling," Everett said. "I'm smiling because it's a beautiful day and I'm walking with the most beautiful woman in town."

"Enough with the nonsense. What do you want?"

Everett laughed. "You never were one to beat around the bush."

"What is it?"

"What makes you think I want something?"

"You know, maybe I will head on back and see what Frank is up to..."

"Okay, okay." He led her through the churchyard and into the cemetery. "Let's go over here, where it's quiet."

"It's quiet here, all right," Nannie said. "And there's a reason. Because no one wants to come here."

"You think so?" Everett cocked his head. "I actually like coming here. It's peaceful."

"It's kind of depressing," she said. But still, she followed him past the first row of graves, marking the resting place of some of the first settlers to the area. The gravestones were starting to crumble, shaded by the branches of an elm tree.

"'For dust thou art, and unto dust shalt thou return,'" Everett said. "I think a reminder of our mortality is a good thing."

"Is this why you brought me here? To remind me that we're all going to die someday?"

"No." Everett scratched at his arm. "I actually brought you here because I heard a rumor that a claw bar was found near the scene of the fire."

"How did you hear that?"

"News gets around. And, well, I hate to cast aspersions, but I think you should know something."

"What?"

"It's about Earl Miller."

"What about him?" They walked through a newer section of the graveyard, threading between headstones. *Beloved daughter. Dutiful wife. Husband and father.* Each soul created by God and missed by those they left behind.

"It didn't occur to me until I heard about the claw bar, but then I realized…" Everett broke off. He loosened his tie and unbuttoned the top button of his shirt.

"What is it?" This was maddening. Why didn't he just say it?

"He has a history of setting fires."

"He what?"

"At the rail yard. He's been caught a couple of times burning things he shouldn't have. Papers one time. Scraps of wood another. It was never—it didn't seem like a big enough deal to terminate his employment, but when I heard about the claw bar... Well, I thought you should know."

Nannie took this in. If it was true, it was another strike against Earl.

But was it true? She looked up at Everett. There was no malice in his eyes. No sense that he was trying to cast doubt on someone besides himself. Still, she couldn't ignore the reality of the situation.

"It's very convenient, you suggesting someone else who could have set the fire," she said.

Everett's jaw set. "Do you still honestly think I would do that to you, Nannie?"

A bird chirped in the poplar tree overhead, and the breeze held just the slightest scent of clover.

"I don't know," Nannie said. "If you didn't set the fire, what were you doing out there?" She couldn't say what she was really thinking. It would be improper. But then, nothing about this situation was proper. "There's only one reason men from town come out on Rocky Ridge Road at night."

Everett's mouth fell open. "I—Nannie—"

She took his agitation to mean he was struggling for words to explain why he had been there.

"I don't drink."

"Gambling, then."

"Not in my nature. I have never gone to Hanson's, and I never will. I don't support establishments of that nature."

She wanted to laugh. It was exactly what any man would say in his position.

"If you weren't visiting Hanson's, and you weren't there to set the fire, I fail to see what reason you could possibly have for being out by our house when the fire started."

Instead of offering an explanation, he said, "What can I do to prove to you I had nothing to do with it?"

Nannie shrugged. "You could tell me what you were doing there."

He bit his lip, took in a long breath, and then let it out slowly. "I did not set that fire. If I figure out who did do it, will that be enough? Or will you still doubt me, even then?"

Nannie looked down. Could she ever really trust Everett? She wasn't sure. Instead of turning back to him, she glanced around at the ground, the headstones, anything. That was when she noticed where they were. *Evelyn Charlotte Turner, 1845-1878*, the headstone read.

"This is your mother's grave." Nannie gestured to the stone.

Everett nodded.

She thought about what he'd said, about how he liked being here. "Do you come here often?"

"As much as I can. It makes me feel close to her again."

Nannie felt the strangest urge to reach out and take his hand. Instead, she raised her face to his and met his eyes. There was an expression she couldn't read there—it almost seemed like tenderness. She quickly looked away.

"If you think I could have set the fire, others must too. Which means I have even more reason to expose what actually happened. Even if it doesn't help you trust me, I'll still help you find out who did this to you," Everett said.

Nannie wasn't sure what to say. She thought about what Molly had said, about how Everett watched her during the service.

"We'll get to the truth together," he continued.

Despite all her misgivings, Nannie liked the way that sounded.

∽ Chapter Eleven ∽

The next few days passed with agonizing slowness. There was no news from the sheriff, and no new leads on the fire. Nannie spent her time working on clearing the land so they could rebuild as soon as they found the arsonist and got paid for the damages. Wednesday morning, as soon as the chores were done, Father saddled Galway.

"Are you going to town again?" Nannie asked. He didn't usually go so often, and she couldn't imagine what he needed today.

"I have a meeting with Warren Campbell," he said. "Bright and early."

"What does Mr. Campbell want?" She got a sinking feeling in her stomach.

"Don't you worry about it," Father said. "It doesn't concern you."

"I'll come too." She stepped toward Kildare's stall and unlatched the gate. "I planned to head into town anyway today."

"What do you need in town?" Father asked as he pulled the leather strap to adjust the position of the saddle.

"I've got the land mostly cleared where the shop was," Nannie said. It had taken her most of the past two days, but she'd done a pretty good job, if she did say so herself. "I was thinking I would go to the lumberyard and see about how much wood we'd need to rebuild."

"Nannie." Father yanked on the strap once more before he dropped his hands. "I don't know if now is the right time to think about rebuilding."

"Why wait?" she said. "The sooner we can get the shop going again, the better. We won't start making money again until it's operating."

"You don't know the first thing about buying lumber," he said.

"That's why I'm going to ask Mr. Wheeler to help me," Nannie said.

"But even if you had the lumber, how would you build it?"

She slipped a halter over Kildare's head and led him out of his stall. "You would have to help me," she said. "I would need you to show me how to drive a nail, and all that, but I'm sure once I had the basics down, it wouldn't be too difficult."

Father shook his head. "It's not that simple, Nan."

"Well then, we'll get help. So many people have told me how sorry they are and asked what they can do to help. We'll take them up on their offer."

Father was quiet for a minute.

"What?"

"I admire your optimism."

"You don't think I can do it."

"It's not that," he said. "It's not you I doubt."

"What do you mean?"

"I don't know how we'd pay for the lumber," he finally said. It was clear it pained him to say the words.

"We'll put it on credit." Every merchant in town was used to farmers using credit at this time of year.

"I don't know, Nan. Even if they will, I think we need to wait."

"Why don't I go down and see what Mr. Wheeler says? I won't move forward without checking with you." She hoisted the saddle into position and pulled the leather straps to tighten it.

Father didn't argue. He just stepped into the stirrup and hitched his leg over Galway's back.

"Maybe while we're there, we can get an update from the sheriff," she said. "Once we know who set the fire, they'll have to pay us what it costs to rebuild, and the money won't be an issue anyway."

"I'm not sure that's how it works," Father said. But he clicked his tongue, and Galway started off. Nannie jumped on Kildare's back and followed just a few paces behind. They were quiet all the way to town.

When they got to Rocky Mount, Father went to the bank to meet with Mr. Campbell, and Nannie headed to the lumberyard on the far side of town. She had tried to get Father to allow her to join him, but he'd put his foot down. So instead, she tied up Kildare and walked inside the wooden storefront of the lumberyard. The small room was lined with shelves displaying samples of different types of wood, and behind, a long open space was filled with planks and boards of various sizes and colors. The whole place smelled like sawdust, and a fine grit seemed to hang in the air.

"Good morning, Miss Starkey." Mr. Wheeler, who ran the place, walked in from the yard. He looked around. "Are you here alone?"

"Yes." Nannie tried not to let her smile falter. She'd only ever been to the lumberyard with Father. Mr. Wheeler was probably not used to seeing young women come in there by themselves. "I want to see about getting some lumber to rebuild my shop. You might have heard that it burned down last week."

"I did hear that." Mr. Wheeler pushed his glasses back with one finger. "I'm very sorry."

"Thank you," Nannie said. "I've cleared the space where the shop used to be, and I'm ready now to rebuild, and I was hoping you could help me figure out what I need."

Mr. Wheeler adjusted his glasses once again. His hair was mostly white and rimmed a bald crown on the top of his head. "Is anyone helping you with this?" he asked, leaning forward to rest his forearms on the counter.

"Father is," she said, hoping to assuage his misgivings. "He had another meeting, or he would be here, but he will help me with the actual building part." Mr. Wheeler was still staring at her, so she continued. "He's very handy, as I'm sure you know. He built that shed last year and fixed the barn when the roof started to leak."

"Right." Mr. Wheeler nodded. "I know he will help you with that. It was more—"

He took in a breath before continuing. "I was really asking, is anybody helping you pay for the wood you'll need?"

"What?"

"It would be quite a large sum," he said. "To buy all the wood to build a new shop. And I just wondered, well, whether you had a way to pay for it."

"No," Nannie said. She tried to sound confident. "But I have some money, and I was thinking I could put the rest on credit."

"That might be a problem, Miss Starkey," Mr. Wheeler said. "I'm afraid your father still owes me for the wood he bought last year for that shed. And for the wood he used to repair your barn."

"He does?" How could that be possible?

"I'm afraid so." Mr. Wheeler's eyes were kind, but his words were firm. "And I'm afraid I can't extend any more credit until I see payment for what your father already owes."

"I see." Nannie bit back the tears that threatened to rise. Had Father suspected this would be the case? Was that why he had tried to keep her from coming here? Were things so bad that they couldn't pay their debts?

"I'm very sorry, Miss Starkey. Especially because of the fire. That was a tough break. But I'm afraid I just can't extend any more credit at this time."

"Thank you, Mr. Wheeler." She turned and walked out before he could see the tears start to fall. As soon as she was outside, she pulled a handkerchief from her pocket and dabbed her eyes. She hadn't realized how dire the situation was. If merchants in town weren't extending her family credit, things were very bad indeed. And without the shop, Nannie had no possible way to help make them better.

Nannie blinked back more tears. She needed to find out who had set that fire. That was the only way this situation was going to get better. If she could prove who did it, she could get reimbursed and she could rebuild. She decided to pay a visit to the sheriff to see if he had an update.

She started to walk toward the town hall, but as she passed Radcliff's, Frank came out and called to her.

"Nannie," he said, smiling. "Just the person I was hoping to see."

She couldn't believe he smiled at her like that, even after she'd rebuffed him after church on Sunday.

"You were hoping to see me?" She tried to keep her voice light. "Why?"

"Because I was hoping to talk to you," he said. "Can we walk?"

Nannie looked around, hoping for some reason to say no. "Don't you have to mind the store?"

"Jimmy's in there," Frank said. "He can handle it for a minute. There's something I want to ask you."

"Oh?"

Frank started walking, and she wasn't sure what to do but follow.

"Nannie, I've been thinking, and I know you're in a tough spot," Frank said. "I know how important that shop was to you and your family. And I was thinking I might have an answer."

"What's that?" She heard her voice shake.

"If you would do me the honor of marrying me, you wouldn't need to rebuild your store," he said. "I could help pay off what's owed, and then I could help your father with the farm, and together I bet we could turn things around. Plus, when we had sons, they would help."

What was he saying?

"Frank, I—" She didn't know what to say. Was he actually proposing marriage?

"Will you?" Frank pulled his hat off of his head and turned it over in his hands. "Marry me, Nannie?"

Nannie was so stunned she couldn't speak. All around her, people walked along the wooden sidewalks, talking, going on as if everything was normal, but Nannie suddenly couldn't breathe. He had actually just asked her to marry him. He had asked her to marry him as a matter of convenience, to save the farm.

"I know it's sudden," Frank said. His cheeks turned a bright shade of pink. "But will you think about it? I care about you, Nannie, and I believe we could be very happy together."

Nannie still couldn't make her mouth form words, and she didn't know what else to do, so she nodded.

"Thank you, Nannie. Think about it, and let me know when you've decided." With that, Frank turned and walked back to the shop, leaving Nannie alone on the sidewalk. She took a few deep breaths, and then, slowly, she began to recover from her shock.

She couldn't believe what had just happened. No, she wouldn't marry him. No, she couldn't. The very thought made her stomach clench. What if he was the one who had set the fire?

But what if he was right and marrying him meant saving the farm? If it was the only way, could she do it then?

She couldn't imagine it. But at least he had given her some time to think about it. She didn't have to accept him—not yet anyway. She still held out hope that they would be able to discover who set the fire. That might still be the key to saving them all.

Nannie turned and marched to the town hall. She had to know if the sheriff was any closer to finding the truth.

But when she asked to see the sheriff, she was told by one of the men that he was testifying at a court case and wouldn't be back for the rest of the day. "Don't you worry your pretty little head about that fire," the man said, his voice dripping with condescension. "The sheriff will take care of it. You just go on home and wait for him to solve the case."

The sheriff might take care of it, she thought as she stepped outside. *But he certainly isn't doing it fast enough.* She wasn't going to "go on home" and wait for him to solve it. She didn't have that kind of time. She needed answers now.

First, there was Frank. Frank, whom she could never marry—could she? Nannie shook her head. There was a decent chance Frank was behind the fire. He'd never accounted for his whereabouts that night, he had a reason to want the store gone, and he'd been seen in the vicinity of the fire with no explanation. He had an injury he tried to hide that could have been caused by the claw bar used to break in.

She also wasn't ruling out Everett. He'd been very charming and convincing, and her heart told her he couldn't have done it, but the heart was sometimes a liar. That was what Pastor Mullins said. Nannie had only ever succeeded by using her head, and her head told her that there were too many reasons Everett could have set the fire to cross him off the list entirely.

And then there was Earl Miller. Earl, who had access to a claw bar and who had made it clear he didn't think her shop should exist. Earl, who had always leered at her. He was the only one she hadn't spoken to.

Well, she was here in town, and she knew where he worked. What would it hurt to go see what he had to say? Before she could change her mind, she unhitched Kildare and rode to the rail yard. She tied the horse up, walked into the little shack, and emerged into the open work area. There were a few men gathered around an engine on the tracks, and another cluster of men, including Earl, bent over the wheel of a boxcar. She approached the second group with as much confidence as she could muster.

"Earl Miller," she announced. Earl looked up and narrowed his eyes when he saw her. "I need to talk to you."

"I'm afraid I can't get away right now," Earl said. He gestured at the train car. "But if you want to send your father to speak to me—"

Fine. If he wouldn't go where they could talk privately, they would have this conversation with witnesses.

"I don't need my father to speak in my place," Nannie said. "I am perfectly capable of speaking for myself, just as I am perfectly capable of running a shop. But as you know, the shop burned down last week, and a claw bar like the ones you have here was found at the scene of the fire. I'd like to know where you were last Monday night."

One of the men next to Earl let out a low whistle. The others watched her, eyes wide.

Instead of answering, Earl laughed. "I don't have to answer your questions." He turned away from her and back to the boxcar.

"Earl Miller, if you don't answer me, it just makes you look guilty."

"If the sheriff wants to come speak to me, he's free to do so," Earl said. "But I'm afraid you need to leave. You can't be here."

"Why, I—"

"Nannie?"

She whirled around and saw Everett hurrying toward her. A man who had been one of the locomotive group earlier was a few steps behind him. He must have gone and told Everett she was here.

"You can't come in here," Everett said. He reached out his hand. "Come on, let's go."

She wanted to argue, but she knew he was right. She really wasn't supposed to be here, she knew that now. And as upset as she was, she saw something comforting in his eyes.

Reluctantly, she took his hand. He laced her arm through his, and though she knew the move was meant to keep her close so he could guide her out, it felt strangely intimate. His arm was strong and muscled, and she could smell the clean scent of his soap.

"What were you thinking, going in there?" he asked as soon as they were out on the street. He dropped her arm. "That's no place for a lady."

"You took me there just last week," Nannie said.

"Yes, but I was there with you," Everett said. "And I needed the metal piece I could only get there. You can't go in on your own. It's dangerous." They started walking toward the railroad office and the station.

"I didn't cause any harm," Nannie insisted.

"Still," Everett said, "it's a good thing I was the one in the office when Barney came running to alert us. If it had been Ned or my father, they wouldn't have been quite as understanding."

"I wouldn't call this understanding," Nannie said. "Dragging me out like that."

"Do you want to know what my father would have done if he'd found you trespassing?" he asked.

"I wasn't trespassing. I wanted to ask Earl Miller—"

"He would have called the sheriff and had you arrested."

"The sheriff is in court. He's unreachable."

"My father would have reached him." The way he said it, Nannie didn't doubt it was true.

"By the way, since you're so interested in Earl, I wanted to let you know I started asking around about him," Everett said. "I hadn't had a chance to tell you what I found out yet."

"Why?"

"Why what?" Some of the agitation had gone out of Everett's voice now, and he just sounded tired.

"Why did you start asking around about Earl?"

"Because I'm hoping that if I help you find out who set the fire, you'll stop thinking it was me."

Nannie mulled his words over. Was he telling the truth? They had walked past the station now. Nannie wasn't sure where they were going, and something in her said she shouldn't be wandering off with a man, but she felt safe with Everett.

"And what did you find out?"

Everett let out a long breath. "Earl has an ironclad alibi for the night of the fire, unfortunately. He was drinking at the saloon all night. Dozens of people saw him there."

"Until how late?"

"Until the bar closed," he said. "At one in the morning."

That was past the time of the fire.

"And you think they're telling the truth?"

"I think it would be hard to get that many people to lie about it," Everett said. "No judge would discount that many witnesses."

"So it wasn't him?" Nannie asked.

Everett shook his head. "I'm afraid it wasn't him."

She saw now where they were going. Up ahead was the bend in the river where they had spent so many summer days catching tadpoles when they were children. Tree limbs arched over the creek bed, dusted with fresh green buds, and the water burbled gently over the river stones.

"So who was it?" Nannie asked.

Everett shook his head, but she got the sense there was something he wasn't saying.

"I haven't been here in so long," Nannie said. She glanced over at Everett, so strong and tall and handsome. It was like looking at a stereoscope, where two images blended into one. She saw him both as he was in that moment—kind, gentle, but possibly dangerous— and as he once was—the wiry, enthusiastic boy who had always greeted her with a smile and pulled her into whatever game he was playing. They'd had so much fun together, so many years ago.

"I come here sometimes when I need to get away," he said. He bent down and scooped the water, which burbled over the small rocks in the streambed.

"Get away from what?" Nannie asked.

Everett shook his head. "All of it."

He was quiet for a minute, and then he straightened up. "Do you ever feel like you don't know what you're supposed to do? Like you don't know what God wants you to do?"

"Yes," Nannie said, thinking of Frank's proposal. Was Frank's offer the answer to prayer she'd been seeking? "It would be so much easier if He made things more clear sometimes." She took a deep breath. His jaw was working again. "Why? What is it?"

The way he looked at her, it almost seemed as if he was thinking something that had nothing to do with fires or rail yards or sheriffs. He took a step toward her, and she almost thought—it almost seemed as if he wanted to—

"I don't know, Nannie," he said with a sigh, and turned away. She felt something inside her shatter. She hadn't realized that she was hoping he thought of her as more than his old friend.

"I should get you back," he said, and she nodded. He was right. Being alone with him out of sight like this could lead to tongues wagging. But she couldn't help the sense of disappointment she felt nonetheless.

As they walked back to the main street in silence, Nannie understood something about herself.

Despite her best intentions, she was falling for Everett.

CHAPTER TWELVE

Long after Nannie had gone to bed that night, she lay awake, tossing and turning. She kept replaying Everett's words in her mind, trying to uncover any hidden meaning or to understand what he meant when he said he didn't know what God wanted him to do. Was he talking about the fire? About her? She also kept thinking about Frank's offer. Was he behind the fire? Could she marry him? If it saved the farm, did it really matter what she wanted?

Finally, Nannie pushed aside the covers and padded down the hallway in her bare feet. Maybe some warm milk would help her sleep. The stove would still be warm enough to take the chill off, even though she couldn't light it at this time of night. She started down the stairs, but as she got closer, she heard low voices. Mother and Father sat at the table, talking. Nannie got to the bottom of the stairs and crept closer, carefully staying out of sight.

"It's time to accept that it's too late," she heard Father say. "If we sell now, Turner says he'll honor the price he quoted back in the fall. No one is going to give us more."

"Is there no other way?" Mother asked.

"I don't see what it would be," Father said. "Warren gave me to the end of the month before he starts the foreclosure proceedings."

"And he won't give you a little grace?"

"He already has," Father said. "Many times."

"But surely there must be something else we can do," Mother said. She was almost pleading.

"I just don't think there is," Father said. "I'll go see Turner tomorrow and tell him that if he closes the deal before the end of the month, the land is his."

"Wait!" Nannie said before realizing she had just exposed her hiding place. Both Mother and Father turned.

"What are you doing up?" Mother said.

Instead of answering, Nannie said, "There has to be something I can do. If we solve the mystery of who burned down the store—"

"I want to know who did that as much as you do, Nan." Father's voice was weary. "But even if we were to solve it, and then we sue, it would take some time for a case to be brought to trial. We wouldn't see payment in time. And even then, we would need a good lawyer, and lawyers don't come cheap."

"Everett would do it." Nannie wasn't sure why she felt so certain, but she did.

"You were sure it was Everett who had set the fire a few days ago," Father said.

"I was wrong," Nannie said. She wasn't sure when she'd crossed Everett off her list, but as the words came out now, she realized she didn't think he was behind the fire. "He couldn't have done it." She didn't know who had, especially if Earl was off the list, but something inside her trusted that Everett was telling the truth.

"Be that as it may, I don't think he could be seen as unbiased," Father said. "And there's no way a trial would happen in time to save the farm anyway."

"Then I'll think of something else." She knew what she had to do. "I can—I'll marry Frank!"

"Frank?" Mother said. "Frank Radcliff?"

Nannie hadn't told them about Frank's proposal. "He asked me to marry him today while I was in town. I'll say yes."

"Why would you go and do that?" Father asked.

"His family has plenty of money. He'll pay off what we owe so we can keep the land. He told me he would. I'll marry him, and then you won't have to sell." She could tamp down any suspicions she still harbored if it would save their land.

Mother looked at Nannie with something like hope in her eyes, but Father shook his head.

"Do you love him?" he asked.

"I—" What was Nannie supposed to say? What did love have to do with it? "I love this land, and I'll do whatever I can to save it," she said.

"I didn't ask if you loved the land," Father said. "I asked if you love Frank. If you do love him, by all means, marry him and make a life with him. But if you don't, this is not something you have to do."

She'd never spoken frankly with her parents about matters of the heart. She also knew theirs hadn't been a love marriage at first but a marriage arranged by the two families. That was how it often worked. She'd always hoped she could marry for love. But that wasn't a luxury most people had around here. Even Molly, who was infatuated with Teddy, was entering a marriage arranged by her father.

"If it will save the land, that's all that matters to me," she said. But even as she said it, Everett's face appeared in her mind. What if Frank wasn't the only option?

But Everett would never—

That was not going to happen.

"Frank Radcliff is a good man," Mother said. The hope in her eyes was almost too much to bear. "And he cares for you."

"Frank Radcliff has had his eye on this land for years," Father said.

"What?" Surely Nannie hadn't heard him right.

"It's true," Father said. "He's made inquiries about portions of the land a few times over the years. Frank is a younger son. He knows his elder brother will inherit the store someday, and Frank is looking out for his own interests. He would love to get his hands on this land so he has something to set him up. If you love him, then that works out perfectly. Marry him, raise a family, farm this land. That way, it won't pass out of the family entirely. But if you don't love him, I can't let you do that, Nannie."

Nannie knew in her heart that she didn't love Frank. She knew she didn't trust him, but more than that, she knew that her heart belonged to another. Still, despite her father's insistence, Nannie wasn't sure that mattered.

"I'll think about it," she said before heading back up to bed.

Nannie thought of nothing else throughout the next day. She didn't see another solution, unless the sheriff managed to figure out who had set the fire. And, as Father had said, even then, it would take time for the case to be brought to trial and the person responsible to be made to pay. She didn't have that much time. They only had until the end of the month. That was less than a week away.

Frank was the only viable suspect left on her list. Earl had an alibi, and Everett—well, she didn't believe Everett could have done it after all. Lenore had seen Frank near the house that night, and he had the motive, and his unexplained injury. She didn't see how he would have had access to the railroad claw bar, but it couldn't have been too hard to find one, and he did have access to kerosene jars. It wasn't looking good for Frank. Still, she thought she could overlook all of that—she'd ask the Lord to help her forgive him—if it meant saving the farm.

By the end of the day, she'd pretty much resolved to take Frank up on his offer.

First thing the next morning, she rode into town. But her first stop wasn't at Radcliff's.

"Are you sure you want to marry him, Nan?" Molly sat on the edge of the settee in the parlor of her house, her eyes wide. "Don't you still think Frank might have been the one who set the fire? You might want to take a few days to consider this before you do anything rash."

"What other choice do I have?"

"Maybe it's not the worst thing in the world if your father sells the land," Molly said. "You could move to town. I'd get to see you more."

"You'll be moving to Richmond this fall."

"But it would be easier to see you when I came back to visit." Molly traced her finger along the vine pattern worked into the cotton print of her morning dress. "I know you feel like you have to do this. You can't see any other way forward," she said. "But maybe this is one of those times when you have to give up and trust that God knows the way even if you can't see it yet."

Nannie knew Molly was right. But she also knew that God had presented her with a perfectly reasonable solution. Maybe it was time to stop dithering and do the thing that made logical sense.

"Promise me you won't do anything drastic just yet," Molly said. "Take a few days to think it over."

"I have thought it over, Molly, and I don't see—"

"Take a few days. Will you please do that?"

She didn't see the point in waiting. Her mind was made up. She had come to town to tell Frank yes. But she knew Molly wasn't going to give in. She was going to nag her until she agreed.

"Fine," Nannie said. "I'll wait a few more days. But I'll be back on Monday to tell Frank I accept."

⚭ Chapter Thirteen ⚭

Nannie spent the next two days at the farm, helping clear out the garden beds for planting. On Sunday, she rode into town with her family and went to church and then spent the afternoon reading and preparing supper. She also started thinking about a cake for Lenore, who would turn nine in a few days. Lenore requested a chocolate cake with vanilla frosting, and Nannie looked through the pantry, checking to see which ingredients they needed. She would need to go to town to buy sugar as well as flour. She could get everything at Radcliff's. Soon, she wouldn't need to buy things from there. As Frank's wife, she would be able to take whatever she needed from the store's shelves.

On Sunday evening, she laid out her best dress, her lavender linen with the ruffles, and also set out her hat with feathers for her trip into town to see Frank the next day. She had worn out her knees with praying, but she hadn't received any other answer. If marrying Frank was the only way to save the farm, she would do so, and gladly.

But just before dinner, there was a knock on the front door. Mother and Lenore looked at Nannie, eyes wide. They weren't expecting any visitors. Father was still out in the barn, so Nannie went to the door and pulled it open cautiously.

Everett stood there. Her heart jumped, and her stomach did a kind of flip-flop. He wore a suit of fine linen and a silk tie under his worsted wool coat. His leather shoes were shined to a high sheen. He looked so out of place on the farm in his fine clothes that she wanted to laugh. But instead, she smiled.

"Hello, Everett." Suddenly, Nannie felt very self-conscious about the state of the house. The roof sagged, the floor was worn, and the paper was peeling. Everything was neat and clean, but it was run-down. Nothing like the Turner place, she was sure.

"Good evening, Nannie. I was hoping I could speak to you."

She started to pull the door open to usher him in, but Everett shook his head. "It's such a nice evening. Would it be all right if we took a walk?" He inclined his head, nodding at Mother and Lenore inside. "Good evening, Mrs. Starkey, Lenore." Mama beamed. Everett turned back to Nannie. "We would stay in sight of the house."

"All right," Nannie said. "Let me retrieve my cloak." She grabbed it and threw it on, ignoring the questioning looks from Mother and Lenore. Then she stepped out onto the porch. The sun was starting to slip below the hills, casting a golden light around the yard and the barn.

"I'm sorry for surprising you like this," Everett said.

"It's all right." If only he knew how happy she was to see him. How her whole body felt lighter, just being next to him. "I'm glad to see you," she admitted.

"You are?" Everett smiled and quirked an eyebrow, and Nannie felt embarrassment flood her. Why had she said that? He wasn't here on a social call.

"What brought you out here?" she asked. They walked across the yard toward the garden. The warblers sang in the trees, and the snowdrops were just starting to emerge. The air held the faintest scent of pine.

"I heard a rumor in town yesterday," he said. "People are saying Frank Radcliff has proposed to you, and you plan to accept."

"Who told you that?" Molly wouldn't have gossiped. She wasn't like that. Had Elsa overheard their conversation and repeated it?

"It doesn't matter how I heard. The point is—"

"It very much does matter," Nannie said. She stopped in her tracks. "Who told you?"

"I talked to the sheriff, and I wanted to let you know what he told me about Frank."

What? "What did he say?" They walked past the garden toward the spot where the store used to be.

"Frank was indeed spotted out this way the night of the fire," Everett said. "There are several witnesses who placed him at Hanson's, including the proprietor herself. He was at the gambling tables all night and lost a good deal of money. I'm told he's been spotted there a lot, trying to win enough money to make up for what Radcliff's has been losing to your shop, but it hasn't gone the way Frank hoped it would, it seems. It never does. I thought you would want to know this about the man you plan to marry."

Nannie bit her lip. So Frank was a gambler.

"He arrived shortly after eight in the evening and didn't leave until after eleven," Everett said. "That was confirmed by several sources independently."

Nannie absorbed the full implication of his words. Frank couldn't have been the man Lenore saw outside her window.

"So Frank does have an alibi for the time of the fire," Everett continued. "He didn't do it. But you can't marry him, Nannie. You can't marry a man like that."

He was right. Even now that she knew he was innocent of the fire, if he was the kind of man who gambled regularly, he would surely lose plenty of money at the tables. There was a chance he would gamble away everything. She'd heard of it happening before. The thought made her stomach turn. But still, there was something that didn't add up.

"What about you? You've never told me what you were doing out here that night."

"I've told you that I wasn't visiting Hanson's," Everett said. "And that's true."

"But what were you doing?"

He took in a deep breath and let it out slowly "I can't tell you that right now, but I promise you can trust me. I'm begging you to trust me."

The thing was, she did. It defied explanation, but she knew she could rely on him. What he was telling her was true. They'd walked to the far end of the yard now, where the scarred and blackened earth had been cleared and all that stood in the place where her dreams used to be was the store's burnt chimney.

"It was Molly," he said, turning to face her.

"Molly?" He couldn't be serious. "Molly set the fire?"

"No." He laughed and shook his head. "No, I'm sorry, I didn't mean that. What I meant was, Molly was the one who told me you were planning to marry Frank."

"What?" What had she been thinking? "Why would she do that?"

"Presumably, to try to get me to stop you," he said.

"Why would she think you could do that?"

Everett laughed again and then sighed. "Because she's not blind. She could see that I'm crazy about you. She told me your plans because she knew that if I let you get away, I would never forgive myself."

Nannie didn't know what to say.

"I love you, Nannie. I expect you know that by now. Molly could see it, plain as day. I can't stop thinking about you. I wanted to wait until we solved this crime to tell you that, but with Molly's news, I knew I couldn't wait." Everett turned to face her and took her hands. "I had to ask you now whether you would have me."

Nannie was so stunned she couldn't make her mouth form words. Was this actually happening? Again? She couldn't be sure she wasn't imagining it. "What?"

"Nannie Starkey, will you marry me?"

A spark shot through her body. Every part of her said *yes*. This was what she wanted. She had fallen for Everett, and she hadn't imagined it when she thought he felt the same way.

But she hesitated. What if this was his way of getting his hands on the farm?

"How do I know you don't just want the land?" she asked.

"I don't care if my father ever finishes that train spur if it means I get to be with you," Everett said. "I will protect your land forever if you'll agree to be my wife."

She glanced at the empty patch of land where the store used to be. The night of the fire, she had never imagined—

But then, Father had said that God works everything together for good. Had this been what God had in store all along? If she married Everett, they could save the land. They could raise a family here. They could be happy.

She looked up at him, and he was watching her with such blatant hope on his face that her stomach flipped over again.

"Yes," she said. "Yes, Everett Turner, I'll marry you."

～ CHAPTER FOURTEEN ～

Everett and Nannie agreed to keep their decision quiet, at least until he had a chance to speak to his father, who would call on Nannie's father to work out the details and make the arrangements. Nannie was so happy she would have agreed to anything. She couldn't believe it—she would soon be Mrs. Everett Turner. When Molly had told her to trust God to provide an answer, who could have imagined this was what He had in mind?

The next day, Nannie rode into town to get the necessary items for the birthday cake for Lenore. Before, she could have easily taken them from the shop, but now she had to go all the way into town to purchase them at Radcliff's. But she needed to speak to Frank anyway. She needed to tell him she couldn't marry him after all. She couldn't marry him, because she was going to marry Everett. She played the scene from last night over again and again in her mind, remembering the moment he had said he loved her. It made her stomach flutter every time. She wasn't sure how she could keep such news quiet for long—surely others must see that everything about her had changed?

In the moments when her mind cleared, and she could manage to form thoughts that didn't revolve around Everett, Nannie was also vaguely aware that she had a dilemma. If Earl Miller had an alibi for the night of the fire, and Frank had an alibi, and she knew

Everett hadn't done it...who had? She was out of suspects and had no new leads. But she couldn't let such thoughts dampen her spirits. The sheriff would find the truth. In the meantime, she would focus on the good news that Everett loved her. She got to town quicker than usual, or at least it felt that way. She had been so lost in her thoughts she barely remembered the journey.

Nannie decided she would go to Radcliff's first and then stop in and see Everett after that. Her whole body tingled just thinking about it.

But first, she had an awkward conversation in front of her. She tied up Kildare and walked into the store, rehearsing in her head the words she would say. It was best to be direct. No need to tell him what she knew, or that she would marry Everett instead. But when she walked up to the counter, it wasn't Frank standing there, but his older brother, Jimmy. The one who would inherit the store. Jimmy had pocked cheeks and blond hair tinged with red, and he always seemed to have a scowl on his face.

"Good afternoon, Miss Starkey." Jimmy nodded at her. "What can I help you find today?"

"I need to buy some sugar and some flour," she said. "And I was also hoping to talk with Frank. Is he available?"

"Sure. Let me help you with the goods, and then I'll go get Frank. He was here a little while ago, but he may have gone upstairs. I'll find him for you." After he scooped out the flour and sugar she needed—*no doubt flour and sugar that came from the shipment I sold to Frank*, she thought wryly—he marked her name down in the accounts ledger along with what she'd bought. Nannie had brought a few coins but preferred to put her small purchase on credit. Once she was married to Everett, she was sure the debt could easily be paid off.

Jimmy had gone out the back door of the store, which led to the stairs to the second floor, where the family lived. Nannie was left alone at the counter. She let her eyes scan the shelves for a while, and then she looked around the shop. She was the only customer in there at the moment. She rehearsed what she would say to Frank while she waited. She would just keep it simple. She was sorry, but she couldn't marry him. No need for further explanation. She didn't want to humiliate him by explaining or belaboring it. Where was he though? This was taking longer than she had expected.

Nannie looked down and let her eyes rest on the account book, where Jimmy had recorded her purchase of flour and sugar and the amount owed. Below her name, on the next line, was a note that E. Turner had bought a large jar of kerosene.

Wait.

Everett had been in here today, to purchase kerosene? She supposed it wasn't all that strange—folks needed kerosene for lamps—but it did seem like he'd bought a large amount. Then she had an idea. Seeing that Frank and Jimmy were nowhere in sight, she pulled the accounts book closer and flipped back through the pages, searching for entries dated in mid-February, before the day of the fire. She ran her finger down the list, looking for purchases of kerosene, and—

Oh. Oh dear. Suddenly, Nannie felt her head grow light and her stomach turn.

The afternoon of the fire, E. Turner had purchased a large amount of kerosene.

She grabbed on to the counter to hold herself up as it suddenly hit her how wrong she'd been. Everett was the one who started the fire after all. She'd been right in the beginning. He had shown up at their door to alert them to the fire he'd set himself so he would look like a hero. He had taken the claw bar from the rail yard himself. He had dropped that cuff link when he broke in to start the fire. He had lied to her from the first moment.

And she had fallen for it. She'd believed that he was helping her, that he cared for her. She felt bile rise up in her throat as she realized that he had played her so easily, that he only asked her to marry him so he could get his hands on the Starkey land. He had told her he would protect her family's land, but she saw now that he intended to do the exact opposite. That was obviously why he wanted to keep their engagement quiet. He wanted to get the deal in writing before they told anyone. Once they were married, he would legally own everything that was hers, including the inheritance of the farm, and then he could do whatever he wanted with the land.

She felt like she was going to be sick.

She wondered how long he planned to wait before he kicked her family off the land and brought the railroad through. He probably wouldn't even wait until the ink on the marriage certificate was dry.

She'd been such a fool. She couldn't believe she'd fallen for his good looks and his smooth words, his good-guy act. She'd truly believed he loved her. It was embarrassing, really, how easy it had been for him. Shameful.

Nannie turned and stormed toward the door. She could deal with Frank later. Right now, she couldn't think about anything but confronting Everett and telling him what she knew. Rage clouded her vision, but she threaded her way through the displays and out onto the street, and then she marched down the road and right into the station office.

Everett was seated at a desk, alone in the room. Well, that was good, but even if anyone else had been around, it wouldn't have stopped what she was about to say. Everett looked up, and his face lit up when he saw her, but his expression quickly turned to confusion.

"Nannie? What's wrong?"

"I'll tell you what's wrong," Nannie said. "I just discovered that the same man who told me he loved me last night, who asked me to marry him, has been lying to me all along."

"What?" He shook his head. "Nannie, I don't know what you're talking about. What happened?"

"You can stop with the lies, Everett. I can see right through them now. I only wish I'd been able to see so clearly before."

"Nannie. Please. What happened?"

"I was just over at Radcliff's, and I saw your name in the account ledger. An E. Turner bought a gallon of kerosene on the day my shop was burned. Did you think I wouldn't find out, Everett? Do you think I'm so dumb I'd never put it together that you were the one who burned down my shop?"

"What did you say?" Instead of anger or defensiveness, he appeared to be confused. But he'd been acting all along—this was just another of his acts. She would repeat herself if she needed to make herself clear.

"I saw the proof right there in the ledger. E. Turner bought a gallon of kerosene the day of the fire," she said.

"Are you sure, Nannie? It said 'E. Turner'?"

"That's what I just said, isn't it?" She threw up her hands. "And then again, today, you bought another gallon. What are you planning to burn down now?" She hadn't thought through the words before they came out, but once she said them, she realized they could be true.

"He bought more kerosene?" Everett's eyes were wide.

"You. I know that it was you—"

But Everett wasn't listening. He bolted out of his chair, grabbed his hat, and ran for the door.

"Don't you run away from me!" Nannie shouted, but he didn't listen. He didn't even seem to hear. He threw the door open and flew out, leaving it creaking on its hinges.

"Everett!" She ran after him, but by the time she got out the door, he was already halfway down the block, running toward the north side of town. She followed after him, and as she ran, she noticed that she wasn't the only one running up Main Street.

That was when she saw the plume of heavy black smoke rising up from behind the buildings. What was—?

The old schoolhouse. Nannie knew instantly.

The old schoolhouse was on fire!

∾ CHAPTER FIFTEEN ∾

By the time Nannie reached the schoolhouse a few minutes later, the building was already engulfed in flames. Dozens of people had gathered around, and some carried buckets, but no one was using the pump in the schoolyard to draw water to try to fight the flames. It was too late. The structure was already nearly consumed.

Where was Everett? She scanned the crowd, searching for him. She saw Mr. Taylor, Mr. Wheeler, Jimmy Radcliff, and even Sheriff Bush, who ran up a few minutes after Nannie, holding his hat on with his hand as he raced toward the fire—but Everett wasn't there. How had he managed it? He must have set the fire and then rushed back to the office to have been at his desk when she came in. He would have had to move quickly, but he could have—

There was a loud pop from inside the schoolhouse, and sparks flew in every direction. The crowd surged back, and she kept scanning, but—

She heard a shout—barely audible over the roar of the flames—from the cleared area by the trees at the edge of the yard. She turned and saw Everett.

Everett, leaning over another man, trying to pin him down. Who was that? What was he doing?

Mr. Taylor also noticed the two men and ran over to see what the fight was about. A few others followed, including Sheriff Bush.

Nannie followed a few steps behind the men. By the time she made it to the group, Sheriff Bush had Everett's arms pinned behind his back and Jimmy Radcliff had—

Nannie sucked in a deep breath when she saw who Everett had been fighting. Jimmy constrained Ned Turner.

"Ned was the one who set the fire!" Everett shouted.

But his words were nearly drowned out by Ned yelling, "Let go of me! He's crazy!"

"It was Ned who set the fire at the Starkeys' store too," Everett cried. He wasn't trying to get away from the sheriff. He didn't seem angry at all. In fact, Nannie thought he struggled to hold back tears.

"He's lying!" Ned, on the other hand, was enraged, straining against Jimmy, trying to pull his arms free. "I had nothing to do with this. Why is he attacking me?"

"Edward Turner, stop lying!" Everett shouted. "We all know you did it!"

Edward. The name floated at the edge of Nannie's consciousness.

"Both of you, come down to the station, and we can work this out there," the sheriff said.

Everett held out his hands willingly for the handcuffs the sheriff held out, but Ned fought harder to get free from Jimmy.

"I'm not going to the station," Ned shouted as the sheriff slapped handcuffs on him. "You can't do this! I'm innocent!"

Despite his protests, Nannie knew that Ned wasn't innocent. In that moment, she realized she'd seen Ned's full name on shipping invoices dozens of times. She'd never paid attention to it, but somewhere in the back of her mind she'd known Edward was his name. Ned was a nickname.

Suddenly she understood how badly she had misjudged everything.

It was Ned. Ned had as much to lose if the Turners didn't sell their land as Everett did. He also had free access to the rail yard and could have easily taken a claw bar. It was Ned—Edward—who had dropped that cuff link inside the shop the night he'd set it on fire. Who'd bought the kerosene from Radcliff's.

She watched as the sheriff and Jimmy took the brothers away from the scene. Nannie wanted to run after them, to talk to Everett, to tell him how sorry she was, but she could clearly see that now was not the time. Instead, she turned back to the schoolhouse, which was slowly being consumed by the flames, another victim of Ned's greed. Once there was no schoolhouse, the Turners would be able to purchase the land that was the last remaining parcel—besides her family's—that they needed to complete the Lynchburg spur.

She stood and watched until the roof fell in, sending up a shower of sparks, and then she decided she couldn't bear to see any more. She headed toward the sheriff's office. She didn't care how long she had to wait. She would be there when Everett was released.

CHAPTER SIXTEEN

It was nearing nightfall by the time Everett was released from the sheriff's custody. Ned remained, locked inside the small cell in the corner of the office. Nannie was pretty sure he would be staying there for quite a while. She had waited on the hard wooden chairs inside the front room for many hours, and she was hungry and tired, but the moment Everett stepped out of the back room and saw her waiting, his face broke into a smile, and she knew it had been worth it.

"Nannie." The corners of his eyes crinkled as he smiled. "You're here."

She stood and clutched her hands together. "I needed to wait for you," she said. "I owe you an apology. I was wrong."

Everett touched her arm. "Let's get out of here," he said. "It's nearly dark. We need to get you home."

They stepped out of the office, dim in the dying evening light, and out onto the street. People walked about, talking to one another quietly. No one paid them any mind as they made their way up the street.

"Kildare is tied up over there," she said, gesturing to the general store. He nodded, and together they walked toward the horse. "Everett, I'm so sorry. I know now it wasn't you who set that fire."

"No, it wasn't," Everett said. "But I can see why you thought it was." His eyes were shadowed, and she knew he was grieving what his brother had done and what it meant. "My father will not be trying to get your land anymore, for what it's worth. I can tell you right now that's no longer in the cards. If the Lynchburg spur is to happen, it will have to go another way."

He helped her up onto Kildare then walked beside her until they reached his horse outside the railyard. Then they started off through the town.

"You think he's going to give up now?" Nannie said. "Why would he?"

"Because he's going to be very busy trying to keep his elder son out of prison. The judge may take a kinder view toward the proceedings if he's willing to make restitution and pay off the debt your father owes on the land."

"Spoken like a true lawyer."

He shrugged. "It's not the worst thing to have one around."

They rode in silence for a moment. She'd had plenty of time to think over the long afternoon, and when she thought back over her interactions with Everett the past couple of weeks, she realized that today's revelations weren't a complete surprise to him.

"How long have you known?" she asked.

"I wasn't sure until today, when you told me about the kerosene," he said.

"But you suspected him, didn't you?"

"It's hard to think that someone you love could do something like that," Everett said. His voice was deflated, pained. "Our father wanted that land, wanted it badly, but it's hard to imagine anyone going to the lengths Ned did to try to get it. Still, when you found that cuff link, that's when I started to wonder."

"It belonged to Ned?" The sound of the horses' hooves beat against the packed earth.

"I hadn't seen it before, or I would have known right away. It seems his wife got him the monogrammed set for his birthday, before I came home."

"But did you ask him about it, when you saw what I'd found?" Nannie said. "Surely you had to have suspected. There can't be that many people around here with those initials."

"I did ask him about it, after Sheriff Bush interrogated me."

"And what did he say?"

Everett shook his head. "He denied everything. Just flat-out said it wasn't his and he didn't know what I was talking about."

"And you believed him?"

Everett took in a deep breath and let it out slowly. "I wanted to, so I let myself."

Nannie let those words settle over her, trying to understand. He loved his brother and wanted to believe the best of him.

"Is that why you were out on Rocky Ridge Road that night?" she asked. "Were you following him?"

"Yes, but—" He broke off. "Marjorie came and told me he had disappeared after dinner, and I suspected he might have headed out to Hanson's. He has always had a taste for liquor, and when he gets to gambling…" He shook his head. "He's lost a lot in recent weeks, and Marjorie was worried. I was hoping to prevent him losing any more of the money he needs to support his wife and children."

"I see." She tried not to cringe. Hanson's sure did a brisk business.

"And I—well, it was stupid, in retrospect, but I thought I might be able to stop him—to, I don't know, talk him out of it. I don't know what I was thinking."

"But his business wasn't at Hanson's," Nannie said.

"Well, he did go there afterward," he said. "That's why I didn't see him coming back down the mountain. And the next day, when I saw him, I asked him what he knew, and once again he denied knowing anything. And, like a fool, I believed him."

"You love your brother." They were out of town now, making their way slowly up the road that wound through the mountains toward home. The golden evening light made the hills glow, and the slow, steady saunter of the horse beneath her was rhythmic and soothing.

"I let that love blind me to things I should have seen sooner," Everett said. "It was the same with your wagon wheel. I was walking down Main Street and saw my brother hurrying away from your wagon. That was when I decided to look it over and saw that broken spoke. I'm not sure why he did it—maybe to distract you from investigating the fire, I don't know. All I know is that when I asked him about it, he denied it, and I chose to believe him. I should have asked more questions. I should have been willing to face the truth, no matter how hard it was."

Yes, you should have, Nannie thought. But if he had, if they had figured out who had set the fire right away, would she have ever spoken to Everett? She might have assumed he was in on it, and that he sided with his brother. She would never have gotten to spend time with him like she had the past few days. She never would have gotten to see that he wasn't her enemy at all. She wouldn't have seen his kind heart and generous spirit. She certainly wasn't thankful for the fire—it was still horrible, no matter how you looked at it—but the Lord had used a terrible situation and had indeed made something beautiful out of it. He had brought Everett into her life and shattered all of her preconceptions about him. He had taught her how to see with her heart, not with her mind.

"Don't be too hard on yourself," Nannie said. "We all do crazy things because of love."

"Oh yeah?" Everett turned his head and grinned at her. "Like what?"

"Like agreeing to marry a man who is impossibly stubborn and ridiculously trusting."

"You'll still marry me, after all this? Even knowing what my brother did?"

"This isn't just your way of trying to get my father's land, is it?" She was smiling, but a small part of her heart was frozen, waiting for his answer.

"Of course not," he said. "I don't care if he gives that land away. I don't care if another foot of railroad track ever gets laid in this city. All I want is to be with you, whether that's at the farm, or in town, or somewhere else entirely. Wherever you are, that will be home to me."

"And Lenore?"

"She will always be a part of our family."

"Then of course I'll marry you, Everett Turner." She smiled. "I may not want to sit across from your brother at family gatherings, but I will love you and be true to you until I die."

"Fair enough." Everett laughed. "I don't know how I got so lucky."

"It's a good thing God knows what we need better than we do," Nannie said.

"You can say that again."

They rode in companionable silence for a moment, each lost in their thoughts. Nannie couldn't believe what had happened in the past few days. She couldn't believe how much had changed and how God had worked beyond her wildest imagination. Everything she thought she knew about how her life was going to unfold had been upended, and she couldn't be happier about it. And God, she suspected, was only getting started.

The setting sun cast the mountains in a glorious orange glow. She couldn't imagine any place more beautiful. She couldn't imagine anyone she'd rather spend these days with. And she couldn't wait to see what God had in store next.

ALL THAT GLITTERS

by

NANCY NAIGLE

Many are the plans in a person's heart,

but it is the Lord's purpose that prevails.

—Proverbs 19:21 (NIV)

∞ CHAPTER ONE ∞

Sacramento, California

Present Day

The words were clear. Grandpa Johnny had passed, but Eliana Turner's mind wrestled with the information.

The man on the other end of the phone was still speaking, but she couldn't process a word he was saying with all the memories and regrets crowding her brain at the moment.

As clearly as if he were standing in the room, she pictured Grandpa Johnny and his broad smile. The way his thick, weathered skin made deep, sunray-like trails from the outer edges of his dancing blue eyes. The shock of wild white hair that scraped his collar and tempted her to flatten it into place.

"I'm sorry. You're going to need to repeat all of that. Can you hold on one moment, please?" Eliana lowered the phone from her ear to her heart, holding it there in both hands.

I was going to come soon. I was away too long. Work. Things came up.

None of that mattered now. The regrets wouldn't bring back another chance to see him.

She inhaled sharply, trying to settle the volley of emotions so she could speak.

"I can't believe he's gone," Eliana said. "I spoke to him less than a week ago. He didn't have a complaint in the world." He never did though.

"I'm sorry for your loss." The attorney from Rocky Mount, Virginia, sounded sincere.

"Thank you for calling." His name had already slipped her mind.

"Well, there's another reason for this call."

"Oh?" The hairs prickled on the back of her neck. "Yes?"

"When can you come and settle the final details of his estate?"

"Me?"

"Yes ma'am. You're the last living relative. If you fly in Wednesday, we can meet Thursday. The funeral is Saturday. I'm sure you're planning to come for that, aren't you?"

"Yes. Of course. I live in California. I'll need to make arrangements. Buy a plane tick—"

"No need," he said. "Your grandfather made provisions for me to send you a round-trip plane ticket. I'll have my office book your flight and car rental. My office, however, is in Rocky Mount. It's not far, but someone can come get you, or I'll meet you in Burnt Chimney, if that's easier."

"I'll find my way to Rocky Mount. I travel for work all the time. I can buy my own ticket too." She was a teenager when her mother moved them away. She hadn't been to Rocky Mount since then, because her visits had been quick check-ins with Grandpa Johnny. There'd never been a reason to go anywhere else but his farm.

"Your grandfather was very specific in his wishes," the attorney said unapologetically.

"And he *specifically* said for you to buy my ticket to Virginia?" It came out snippy, and she hadn't intended that, but before she corrected her tone, he was already talking.

"Yes. He did. Specifically. There's the matter of the house too."

"I'm sorry. Your name again?" She picked up a pen and pulled a pad of paper over to take notes.

"Nelson Luther. I'd like to get through all the paperwork and arrangements as he requested, unless you'd rather—"

"No. Of course. This was… You caught me off guard. I didn't expect…" A single tear slid down her cheek. "I'll be at your office next Thursday."

Mr. Luther gathered her information for the plane ticket. "That should do it. I'll get the flight itinerary to you this afternoon."

"Is there somewhere you recommend staying nearby?" she asked.

"I'd suggest staying at your grandfather's house. If all goes to plan, it'll be yours anyway. Key is under the—"

"Milk can." She finished his sentence. "I remember." That was one of the best things about Grandpa Johnny. Nothing ever changed. Not until now.

"That's right. I'll see you next week."

She ended the call. Loneliness hung over her shoulders as heavy as if someone had flung a load of blankets on top of her.

She'd known loss. Both the physical and emotional kind. After her parents divorced, she didn't see Dad for years, and she'd been a daddy's girl. For a long time, she believed he didn't love her anymore.

When she was a little girl, Dad had been the one who gave hugs. She always felt so safe with him, but once Mom took her to the West

Coast, those ties were severed. When they got to California and settled in, Mom had zero tolerance for any discussions about Eliana's father.

The landscape was beautiful in California's wine country, but she missed Burnt Chimney desperately. She quickly learned that her mother's family wasn't warm and loving like Dad's. She never wanted for anything, but all the pretty clothes and the big house on the vineyard wasn't enough to make up for the icy emotions that hung between her mother and the family. Eliana stayed to herself, studied hard, and went straight to college, anxious to be on her own.

Mom became more high-strung and demanding over the years. Still angry on her deathbed, she'd insisted Eliana never talk to anyone in "that family."

But Eliana had broken that promise years before.

She'd reconnected with her father and Grandpa Johnny while away at college. Too many missing pieces of the story didn't make sense to her adult mind. She needed to understand what truly transpired back in Burnt Chimney. She was thankful she had braved contacting Dad and asked the hard questions.

After a year of phone calls and explanations, she'd agreed to visit. Thank goodness she had too, because it wasn't but a few months afterward that Dad died in his sleep. It was the first funeral she ever attended. The black dress she'd bought to wear to it still hung in her closet. Never worn again.

She and Grandpa Johnny became closer, and she clung to those pieces of her past, when the days were fun and there was so much space to run and play.

Whenever her work took her to the East Coast, she made time to stop in her old hometown and stayed connected through phone calls and good old-fashioned letters. Grandpa Johnny loved letters.

She glanced at the calendar and circled today's date, May 1. Her life was pivoting again. Dad was gone. Mom was gone and now Grandpa Johnny too.

May Day. May Day. I'll miss you the most, Grandpa Johnny.

Burnt Chimney, Virginia

The next Wednesday, from the first-class window seat on her flight from Sacramento to Virginia, Eliana watched the changing terrain.

The first-class ticket had been a pleasant surprise, since she normally flew coach for work. Usually working on last-minute updates on the way to her assignment.

In first class, she had room to open her laptop with no concern for the guy in front of her leaning back, but she hadn't even taken her computer out of her bag on this flight. It was kind of nice staring out the window at the scenery and, honestly, after the news of Grandpa Johnny's passing, she wasn't motivated to work.

She remembered Grandpa Johnny complaining about how much she worked. "If you don't slow down and enjoy some of what's going on around you, Eliana, you're going to wake up old and tired, with no memories at all."

Today, those words held more weight. They weren't the ramblings of an old man but rather messages of hope from a loving grandfather. It was heartbreaking that she'd never hear his wisdom again.

His deep voice, strong and unwavering, always brought her joy. A phrase she hadn't heard him use since she was a kid popped into her mind. *"Some folks believe there's nothing more useless than a single cuff link. But even that is worth more than you can imagine."*

It was a saying referring to the cuff link that had sat under glass on Grandpa Johnny's mantel for as long as she could remember. The one she'd been forbidden to touch. Shiny and real gold, like a treasure. One with elegant scrolling letters that made it hard to make them out.

Why he'd kept that gold cuff link under glass never made sense to Eliana. It just looked like an old button to her. She'd dreamed that it was worth a lot of money. For years, princess dreams of being the heiress to priceless heirlooms had danced in her mind. Perhaps even a cuff link crown, but Grandpa Johnny's face when she brought up the subject made it seem like a taboo subject, so she'd kept her questions to herself.

There's no chance to ask now.

The airline attendant made one last pass as the final-approach announcement came over the speaker.

It wasn't long after that the tires screeched on the runway and the plane slowly taxied to the gate. It didn't take any time to make her way through the small Richmond airport with her carry-on to the rental car counter.

She carried the keys and paperwork out to the lot where a compact car that looked more like a brightly colored jelly bean sat in the parking space that matched the number on her paperwork. *Good thing I didn't bring a large suitcase.* She might have had to seat belt it in the passenger seat for it to fit.

That was one perk of traveling for work. She'd become quite adept at packing light. The dress for the funeral was rolled up in the bottom of her bag, and she'd been able to fit in some mix-and-match things to get her through the short stay.

Eliana exited the parking garage and then floored it to merge onto the interstate. The car whined, struggling to keep up with traffic, but once she got out of the city limits, the traffic thinned out and neighborhoods dotted the landscape fewer and farther between.

An hour west of the city limits, green pastures of cattle replaced the buildings and cars. She slowed to take a turn. Cows looked her way from the fence line.

Did that cow just nod at me?

She let out a long breath. Maybe it was easier to slow down when surrounded by wide open spaces.

It was beautiful countryside. She couldn't argue with that.

Spring colors were everywhere. Hot-pink crepe myrtles bloomed as bright as a highlighter on homework in front of a soft yellow brick ranch next to a field of cows knee-deep in tender grass.

Memories of Grandpa Johnny watching livestock for their first few days on a too-green pasture lest they get upset stomachs filled her mind.

He'd say, *"They're like kids in a candy shop. They don't know when to stop."*

That still made her laugh, because really, was there ever too much candy? Not even on Halloween, when her parents would take her treat bag and separate the chocolates from the hard candy, doling out a piece or two a day. It hadn't taken her too many years to learn to sneak her own little stash of goodies to please her sweet tooth.

The last time she saw Grandpa Johnny, she'd been managing the opening of a store in Charlotte, North Carolina. She'd driven up for a quick visit, not even staying overnight.

Has it been two years? She counted the months off on her fingers. Sure enough, it had.

She shook her head, saddened that she'd let that much time slip by. It was easy to fall into the rigors of work life—not that it left much of any other kind of life. Her commitment had rewarded her with promotions and a good salary, but she did get lonely.

Grandpa Johnny tried to warn me.

Today was only the second time she'd driven to Burnt Chimney from the Richmond airport. Usually, she came south from DC or from North Carolina. That first visit had been while she was still in college, and that was her last encounter with her father before he died.

She'd avoided Mom's questions about her whereabouts twice that month, both about the visit and Dad's funeral not long after. She struggled over keeping the secret, but ultimately there was no getting Mom to ease the hate in her heart for the Turner family. It was a relief that there was no one left to keep the secret from.

Vast warehouses, and even a solar farm, made wide swathes interrupting what used to be miles of farmland. But the closer she got to Burnt Chimney, the quieter things became.

The goat farm where her third-grade class had taken a field trip was still there. She slowed, laughing at the way the field seemed alive because it was kidding season. Baby goats leaped and climbed on top of their tired mothers chewing their cud. The goats were so cute when they'd been allowed to bottle-feed them. She was half tempted to swing in for an up close peek, but she wanted to get to the house before dark.

Finally, she passed the sign welcoming her to Burnt Chimney.

She passed the creamery and post office. They hadn't changed since she was a little girl. There was no Main Street in Burnt Chimney, but there was a tanning salon on the main route now, which seemed extraordinarily out of place.

There was also a new gas station with nearly a dozen pumps, diesel fuel, and a convenience store. That sure beat the nearly thirty-minute drive it used to take Mom to go to town just for a loaf of bread when they lived here.

"Life is a lesson in keeping perspective and your priorities straight." That was what Grandpa Johnny always said.

He never said one negative word about Mom, even though her destructive behavior deserved more than a few for the way she'd treated the Turner family. It had embarrassed Eliana to learn the mistruths her mother had drilled into her head as a young girl. One thing was for certain: Mom's recollection had been distorted.

Thank goodness I finally learned the truth.

Her GPS announced her destination was ahead on the right. She slowed and turned down the dirt lane.

Dust kicked up behind her, billowing around the tiny car as she pulled to a stop in front of the house. She didn't get out right away. Instead, she stared at the front door, praying Grandpa Johnny would walk out and open his arms. Wishing the call about his death was all a mistake.

It was still. And quiet. She got out of the car, walked up to the porch, and sat in one of the white rocking chairs that lined it like soldiers on guard. One rocker positioned between each wooden porch post, with a side table in between. She scooted back in the chair and pressed her toes against the deck boards to rock.

She texted Nelson Luther to let him know that she'd made it to town and would meet him at his office in the morning. No response.

She set her phone on the arm of the chair and walked around to the side of the house. The old rope swing still hung from the big sweet gum tree. She walked over and tugged on the thick rope, wondering about the safety of the thing. Sweet gum pods littered the ground. She remembered how they'd bruise her feet when she landed on them. She picked up one of the spiny gumballs and rolled it between her palms. It didn't seem to matter what time of year. They were always under foot.

The sound of a vehicle coming up the driveway sent panic through her. Nelson Luther had assured her no one else would be here. She ducked behind the pump house, quietly chiding herself for being afraid. Maybe it was Nelson Luther checking in.

She watched from her hiding place.

The truck pulled to a stop only a few feet from where she stood.

A man dropped to the ground from the cab in work boots.

Eliana doubted the Rocky Mount attorney would show up in dusty boots and a four-wheel-drive pickup truck. Especially one with a shiny diamond-plate toolbox in the bed.

Her heart hitched when she grabbed for her phone in her back pocket and it wasn't there. She'd left it on the porch, and the closest neighbor was too far away to hear her if she screamed, even on a perfectly quiet spring day.

❧ Chapter Two ❧

Camron Carter was surprised to see a car in Johnny Turner's driveway when he came to water the plants. No one had any reason to be here, as far as he knew.

He walked up to the front door cautiously. He rapped his knuckles on the glass in a quick double-knock. "Hello? Anyone home?"

He listened intently for a scuffle from inside, but there was none. He'd heard about people descending on a deceased person's possessions. It wouldn't be anyone from around here though. If there was one thing he was certain of, it was that everyone in Burnt Chimney and at least three connecting counties respected Johnny.

Johnny had been his best friend, although many considered it odd, since there was a two-generation gap between them. He missed him already.

Something swished in his peripheral.

He spun around and spotted a woman a good foot shorter than himself. Their eyes locked. She lifted her fist in the air. "Who are you?"

He flinched, but when he noticed the pine cone clenched in her hand, he chuckled.

"What are you doing here?" She seemed in a panic. "Answer me." She raised her other hand.

He put his hands on his hips. "What are *you* doing here?"

Her brows furrowed, and she launched a pine cone at him.

He swerved, but it caught him on the ear. "Ouch! Stop." He rubbed his ear.

"You clearly have no business here." Her jaw set, she flung the other pine cone in his direction.

He jumped out of the way. "What the—" He looked over at the crazy woman, and when his eyes met her crystal-blue ones, so much like Johnny's, his mind put together the unmistakable resemblance to the first girl he'd ever fallen in love with.

"Eliana?" He stepped closer. Her auburn hair fell across her right brow. Not bangs like she wore when they were kids, and a darker shade than he remembered, but just as shiny.

She stepped back. "What…?" She cocked her head. "You know who I am?" She stood there, sort of panting. Suddenly, she raised her hands to her mouth as her eyes flew wide. "Oh no. You're Nelson Luther?"

He snickered. "Not a chance." He tugged his ball cap lower on his head. "I didn't mean to startle you, but why were you hiding in the bushes?"

"I wasn't. I'd walked around to the side and realized my phone was on the porch. I was being cautious."

"Well, you're safe, and welcome back to Burnt Chimney. No one told me you were coming."

"And why would they?" Her eyes filled with questions, and he realized she really didn't recognize him.

"It's me. Camron. We went to school together."

She didn't look convinced.

"We used to play right here. Remember in the first grade, when I officiated your wedding to Mike Larkin? You've got to remember that. He wasn't good enough for you, you know?"

"Oh my goodness." She covered her face with her hands. "I'd for-gotten all about that. We were on the sidewalk in front of his house."

"Yeah, and you wore a tablecloth for a wedding veil."

"I did!" Her features softened. "Jelly?"

"No one has called me Jelly in over twenty years."

"Sorry, but you could put away more jelly toast than anyone."

"I've cut down on the sweets since then."

"Of course you have. Sorry. But I can't believe it's you."

"I guess I'm lucky you didn't punch me in the gut like you did Mike when he tried to kiss you on your wedding day. I got off easy with the pine cones."

"Sorry about that." She studied his face. "You look okay. Nothing's bleeding." She winced. "Mike's got to be relieved he didn't *really* marry me that day."

"No. With three divorces under his belt, he probably wishes that marriage to you had counted. You were the only one out of all of them who would've been able to keep him in line."

"Goodness gracious. Three divorces? I guess the third time's *not* the charm."

"Not in his case."

"How have you been?" They walked toward the porch. "You never left Burnt Chimney?"

"I've been good. I left for a while. Went to college. Worked for a corporate farm, but ultimately office work made me miserable.

I came back to what was always in my heart, and that was working side by side with my grandfather and eventually taking over his dairy farm."

She turned and smiled. "Do y'all still make that amazing ice cream?"

"It's even better."

"Impossible."

"Nope. I can prove it to you while you're in town."

Eliana nodded. "I'll take you up on that, but I won't be here long. I'll be heading home after the funeral."

Too bad. She was as pretty as he remembered. His heart hadn't forgotten her. That was certain by the way it was pounding. "It's good to see you. I'm sorry it's under these circumstances."

"Me too. I just spoke to him last week. He sounded fine. Never even mentioned he was ill."

"He wasn't. Not that anyone knew of anyway. It all happened so fast. I was here when he suddenly struggled to catch his breath. I called 911, and the ambulance got here quick. They said he was doing okay by the time he got to the hospital, but that night he was sleeping when the machines went crazy. The second heart attack was more severe. They acted quickly, but they couldn't..."

She looked struck. "I hope he wasn't in pain."

"I hope not too. I don't think he was." Camron's eyes watered. "We were really close. He's been my mentor on the farm. A day didn't go by that we didn't speak."

"I didn't know."

"Yeah. We shared a lot of meals." He choked on the last word. "Here."

"He was a better cook than my grandmother," she said.

"He was, and the smartest man I've ever known. I learned more from him in casual conversation than all the years in college studying this stuff."

A tear slipped down Eliana's cheek.

"You were his favorite subject," Camron said, hoping her tears wouldn't trigger his own. "He was always showing me pictures and telling me what you were up to. He was so proud of how successful you are. I guess that must sound kind of weird to you."

"A little. He mentioned a Camron, but I never put Camron and, well, you, together. You were always Jelly to me. I assumed Camron was some old man from church."

"I'm pretty sure I'm the only Camron in these parts. It's okay. It's been a long time." But Camron remembered everything about Eliana. The scar that was probably still on her left knee from when she fell off the monkey bars on the playground in second grade. The time she burned her hand with a sparkler at the Fourth of July picnic. And that she was allergic to cats but loved them.

"I'm thankful you were here with him when…it happened."

"I'm glad I'm here now." He watched her for a moment, feeling a strange comfort with her even though it had been years since they'd seen each other. "I come over to water the azaleas for Johnny twice a week. He got tangled up in the water hose twice. A few weeks ago, I found him on the ground and offered to do the chore for him. He didn't argue."

"He was never one to complain."

"No, and I would've never suspected he struggled with that task. I was relieved, and a little sad at the same time, that he let me step in. I made a deal with him. I'd water the plants if he fixed us tuna sandwiches." He shrugged. "He accepted the offer without so much as a grumble."

Eliana pulled her hands to her hips. "Wait. You don't expect me to make you a sandwich, do you?"

"Only if you want to."

"I just got here," she said. "I don't know if there's anything in the cupboards."

"There's always something in Johnny's cupboards. I'll make the sandwiches. I know my way around his kitchen."

"That's not necessary," she said.

He walked right by her. "I don't mind at all. After all, you said you just got here, and even the closest airport is a drive. Take a seat in one of those rockers out front, and I'll bring lunch out to you. It'll be like the old days." Camron walked inside. It didn't take him five minutes to whip up tuna salad sandwiches on toast and two glasses of sweet tea.

He kicked the screen door open with the toe of his boot and carried a sheet pan out with the sandwiches and drinks on it. "Here we go."

"Looks like you've done this before."

"Yeah, like I said, we shared a lot of meals."

"Thanks." She lifted half a sandwich from the tray and took a bite. "Mmm. That's pretty good."

"Sandwiches are sort of my specialty."

They ate in awkward silence until Camron shoved the last bite into his mouth and got up. "You'll have to let me know when you want to go to the creamery for that ice cream. I'd love to give you a tour of the place. I've done a lot of expansion."

"I was just kidding about that. I'll be back in California before you know it."

He hoped not. "I never pictured you as a California girl."

She straightened. "Why not?"

The tone in her voice was enough to change the subject. He shrugged. "You'll be comfortable here. Everything in the house is in working order. We redid the guest room over the winter. Johnny hated not having a project, and he'd planned to have a couple of Ag majors from Virginia Tech spend the summer here to earn some work credits. I guess I should make sure someone calls Tech about that and the situation here."

"I could see him taking in college students. He loved teaching people about the land."

"He did, and he wouldn't let me pay him for all the consulting he gave me about my business, so I did things around here to even the score."

"That was sweet of you to spend so much time with him."

"I didn't do it to be nice. We were friends, Eliana. Real friends."

"I didn't mean to suggest otherwise." She stood.

He could see she was irritated. Maybe she was a little jealous of his relationship with Johnny. *Well, that's her problem. She should've thought about that before she stayed away all these years.* She'd been his first heartbreak. Her mom had whisked her away without so much as a goodbye, and he'd never gotten the chance to tell her how crazy he was about her.

Choosing his words carefully, he said, "I know you have an important job and all, but around here, we take care of each other. It's not fancy, but it's a friendly community full of hardworking people, and before you get yourself all in a twist, I'm not suggesting you don't work hard. Johnny said you're one of the hardest working people around. He used to say that was your, and *my*, biggest flaw. That we work so hard we'd never make the time to stop and have a family."

She stood there, staring at him. "He's right." She sat back down in the chair. "I was thinking about that the whole ride here, that I didn't have time for this, but it's the most important thing I have to do right now. Family and all."

"Having the right perspective isn't always easy." Camron wondered if she'd heard that same speech from Johnny. The light in her eyes told him she had.

"Yes," she whispered. "I'm still a work in progress on perspective and priorities, I guess."

She still made his heart race. Camron stepped off the porch and picked up the hose to water the plants. "Aren't we all?"

∿ Chapter Three ∿

"You don't have to do that. I can water the flowers," Eliana said to Camron.

"I know you *can*, but I'm here now, and I've been doing it. I want to. Please let me do it."

She turned her attention to the front door of Grandpa Johnny's house. She swallowed back emotion as it dawned on her that he'd never be there to greet her again.

No big bear hug. No old joke that would make her laugh a week later when she recalled it. No warm-from-the-oven Johnny Pops, which was what she'd always called his famous popovers, although she hadn't had one in years.

Even when Granny Mae was alive, Grandpa Johnny did most of the cooking. Having been a cook in the army, he'd always fix more food than even a big family could consume, so Granny Mae had specialized in serving up leftovers and been happy to do it.

Unlike her parents, Grandpa Johnny and Granny Mae had a peaceful balance in their marriage that made life look so easy. Something she dreamed of having one day.

She sat there staring at the old farmhouse, thinking of how different the time spent here was from when she was with her mom in California. Her dad never seemed as happy as he was when they were here at his parents' house. The same house he'd grown up in. She'd always felt the same way.

Since the early 1800s, Grandpa Johnny would say in his heavy Southern accent when asked how long this land had been in the Turner family.

The house seemed lonely today. There wasn't a single chicken scratching at the dirt out front. What had happened to them? She didn't have the strength to inquire. Emotion hung in the back of her throat, making it hard to swallow, much less ask the question.

She'd grown up just down the street a couple of miles, but most of the time she rode the bus straight here from school because the bike ride uphill to get to the farm was a killer.

I wish you were still here, Grandpa Johnny.

The wine-colored Sweet Williams perked up as Camron slowly made his way around the house. Her love for flowers had started right here in this yard. Memories returned... Picking the perfect blossoms to take inside to Granny Mae, who acted as thrilled as if she were being handed a Miss America cascade of roses no matter how wilted and wild the assortment was. Picking buttercups with Penny to test each other to see if they still loved butter then daisy-chaining them together into matching wreaths to wear on their heads like flower girls.

She rocked back. So many wonderful memories danced in her mind. *Granny Mae used to sit in this rocker and read to me.* Sitting cross-legged, Eliana would get lost in the stories Granny Mae would read, but what she loved most were the ones that Grandpa Johnny told. He made them up, never telling the same one twice. He swept her off on wonderful journeys to faraway lands where good prevailed and the princess lived happily ever after.

I should have written those stories down or asked him to. They'd have been a treasure. Something to share with her own children someday.

That thought made her laugh. She wasn't marriage material. And even if she were, it wasn't likely she'd ever get married and have children when she couldn't even find time for a date. With the hours she worked, and the company's strict "no dating coworkers" policy, her options were slim pickings. The only person she saw with any regularity was the UPS man.

She smiled as she imagined her UPS man riding up on a big brown horse instead of that noisy truck, knocking on her door, scanning her hand with his little machine, and inviting her to ride off into the sunset.

Good looking, great manners, and always on time. Maybe that isn't such a bad option.

She wasn't complaining though. The company had been good to her. Her former position as West Coast Rebranding Executive had been a big deal. Managing the activities that led to the grand reopening of every Mattie's Boutique on the West Coast was a huge undertaking, but she had loved the challenge. Motivating the existing staff as they worked together to achieve the new look was exhausting, but she was good at it.

After three years in the position and opening dozens and dozens of stores on time and budget, she had been promoted to management. Now she supervised other rebranding executives and watched them do the most exciting part of the job.

With her new position requiring about seventy-five percent travel, Eliana sold her car and was at home so infrequently she'd even rented her apartment to people on football game weekends for tidy little sums.

Over the last year, she'd built a great team of highly motivated professionals, and now that the eight new stores in Arizona were up and running, her schedule was a lot more manageable for the next few months.

Eliana had known early on that she wanted a career. She found a job straight out of college and started separating herself from her controlling mother in search of her own identity and the truth.

Grandpa Johnny never spoke a bad word about Mom, but Eliana remembered Mom saying that Dad's parents had always disapproved of her. Eliana never had the guts to ask Grandpa about that. Although now, as an adult, she could understand how no parent would want to see their child mismatched like her mother and father were. Dad had been a hard worker, and Mom, well, she grew up being catered to, and she never was a partner. It wasn't just with Dad. That had become clear by the way she acted in California.

Eliana watched Camron move through the yard with the hose, taking his time and making sure every plant got what it needed.

She got up and walked over to the front door. Her fingers rested on the old metal knob. It had probably been considered quite fancy in its day. Now it wore scars from years of service. She opened the door and stepped inside.

Grandpa Johnny had been a creature of habit, so she expected everything to look the same even though Camron had mentioned some projects. But, to her surprise, everything was different.

Camron must have repaid a lot of consulting hours over the past year.

The living room had a fresh coat of paint that held the softest hint of color. The furniture was all new, except for Grandpa Johnny's old leather recliner. It was so worn that it looked like he'd just stood up from it. She walked over and pressed her hand in the center, where the leather was stretched thin. No one ever sat in that chair but him.

A light-colored area rug was a new addition. It accented the stone fireplace nicely, making it a real focal point behind the jet-black woodstove insert.

She'd have to find new owners for a lot of this stuff. The thought of having an estate sale seemed impersonal. Hopefully, Nelson Luther had detailed instructions. With any luck, as good a planner as Grandpa Johnny was, he might have already outlined an entire inventory with a division of property.

That would be just like you. She lifted her chin and smiled, feeling as if he'd know what she was thinking.

In the kitchen, the long wooden table where they'd gathered for Sunday suppers still took up nearly the whole room. Nothing was more important to the Turners than family, and on Sundays everyone had lent a hand in the preparation of the meal.

It wasn't uncommon in those days for the ten-seat table to be filled, overflowing to card tables in the living room or, when the weather was nice like today, to the porch, where there was space for more guests. She could almost hear the happy hum of activity of those Sundays.

Burnt Chimney life was different from anything she'd experienced since.

Parched from the long day of travel, Eliana filled a glass with water.

The white metal kitchen cabinets had been replaced with beautiful cherry shaker-style cabinets that went clear up to the ceiling. An accent wall in an updated turquoise surprised her, although it probably shouldn't, because Grandpa Johnny had loved turquoise. He'd worn a watch band with turquoise and coral chips embedded in it.

She took a quick look in the refrigerator. All the essentials were there, including coffee creamer still good for another week. Above the old drip coffee maker, she found a full tin of coffee and a sugar bowl.

She ran her fingers over a pack of crackers from the wooden bowl on the counter. A staple from as far back as she could remember. Grandpa Johnny was not above eating a pack of crackers in the field for lunch. Anytime, for that matter. He was pretty low maintenance. Maybe that was the key to happiness. He'd always been the happiest person she'd ever known.

When she returned to the living room, she could see Camron through the front windows coiling the hose over his toned biceps.

It hurt her feelings that Camron had a long friendship with her grandfather, but she had no one to blame but herself. *I should be thankful Camron and Grandpa Johnny were so close.*

But she wasn't. She was definitely a little envious.

CHAPTER FOUR

Eliana walked back outside just as Camron hung the coiled hose on its hook on the side of the house.

"Anything I can do for you before I leave?" He stomped the dirt from his boots.

"No. Thanks." She popped the trunk on her rental to get her suitcase.

Camron was on her heels. "I've got that."

She stepped out of his way but not without saying, "I'm not helpless."

"I'm well aware of that." He heaved her suitcase out of the car and took it up to the porch. "I'll let you take it from here." Then he turned and headed for his truck. He waved from the driver's seat as he drove off.

She stood there until the house phone rang. Eliana ran inside and snatched the receiver from the wall. "Johnny Turner's residence."

"I heard about Johnny passing. This is Gladys, over at the library. Don't you worry, I'm not calling about his overdue books, just wanted to see what we can do to help. The Friends of the Library want to make some casseroles. Is this his granddaughter?"

"Yes, this is Eliana." She made a mental note to look for library books. "Please tell them I appreciate the thought, but I don't need a thing. I won't be in town long enough to put them to use, and I wouldn't want them to go to waste."

"I see."

"If anything comes up, I'll be sure to let you know, Gladys. It's kind of you to call. Thank you."

"Just a few prayers, then," Gladys said.

"I appreciate that."

"Your grandfather, he was good as gold. Everyone loved him. We are very sorry for your loss, but we're all very happy to know you're in town."

Only for a few days, she mentally repeated. She had a life back in California, but that wasn't for her to get into with strangers on the phone.

She hung up. The stretched cord twisted then dangled like a curling ribbon from a balloon.

The words "good as gold" echoed, causing her to turn toward the fireplace mantel.

Gold. She remembered how Grandpa Johnny would never let her touch his special gold cuff link, saying it was an important family treasure.

She walked over to the mantel. The golden cuff link was still there. The domed glass over it appeared to be nothing more than a cheap jelly jar. Funny how different things looked through the eyes of a child. The thick chunk of wood that the glass sat on held a saying. Someone, maybe Grandpa Johnny himself, had handwritten in ink, *Some would say there is nothing as useless as a single cuff link.*

Her cell phone rang. The smiling face of her coworker and neighbor Jan beamed back at her. Eliana swept her finger across the screen to answer. "Hi! How are you?"

"I'm calling to make sure you made it there." Jan's voice always sounded like champagne. Bubbly and light. "How was your flight?"

"The flight was fine. I'm here at the house."

"Great! So you're halfway done."

"We'll see. I have an appointment with the attorney. I sure hope we can get everything squared away fast. I don't want to be stuck here extra days."

"Not the end of the world. You're way overdue for a vacation. Make the best of it."

"I only packed a few outfits," Eliana said.

"So, shop."

"In Burnt Chimney? Jan, you have no idea how small a town we're talking about."

Jan giggled. "There's got to be somewhere to shop."

"Not even a Walmart." Eliana sighed. "I'll have to make it work if our meeting is postponed. It's peaceful here, which is sort of a nice change. I guess I could use a little rest."

"There's nothing on your work calendar that can't wait."

"I turned in my final reports last week," Eliana said. "The team is working on the next round of reopenings in the Northeast. Everything should be fine."

"I'll keep track of them," Jan said. "Don't worry."

"Maybe I'll take a tourist's view of Burnt Chimney and the surrounding areas. It's been a long time since I lived here."

"Get a massage or a pedicure. That's always nice."

"Again. Small town. There aren't an abundance of options here."

"Well, ask around," Jan said. "Those people have to do something for fun. Call me tomorrow with an update."

"Will do." Eliana ended the call. With hesitation, her fingers hovered over the forbidden heirloom. *Why am I acting like I'm going to get into trouble?*

She lifted the glass. The antique cuff link didn't seem quite as shiny as she remembered. She picked it up. It was heavy for being so small, and the scrolling letters still looked as graceful as she'd imagined. Moving to the window for better light, she examined the fine craftsmanship of the scrolling design. It was intricately engraved.

A knock on the front door startled her, and the next thing she knew, the glass dome was bobbling and she was juggling it and the cuff link. The glass hit the floor first, sending splintered shards across the room, followed by the cuff link.

Another knock came. This time much louder.

∾ CHAPTER FIVE ∾

The front door of Grandpa Johnny's house burst wide open, followed by a blustering voice that shook her. "Everything okay in here?"

Eliana froze at the sight of the biggest man she'd ever laid eyes on standing in Grandpa Johnny's front doorway.

His ball cap was pulled so tight to his skull that he looked a bit like a bullet with a fluffy beard nearly down to the middle of his chest. "What broke?" he demanded.

"I—I dropped something. I'm Johnny Turner's granddaughter." There was no way she had a chance against a man that size. "Who are you?"

The man relaxed. "Eliana? Well, I'll be." A wide grin made him suddenly look like a big teddy bear rather than the Hulk. "Hadn't heard you were coming to town for the funeral."

That stung. She stood there, hesitant to let her guard down.

"But of course, you would," he recovered quickly. "I'm sorry you weren't able to be here before…well, before this. He talked about you all the time."

"Should I know you?" This was becoming a trend.

"I grew up a little since you lived here, huh? It's me. Reed."

"You did grow up, and it looks like you never stopped!" She knew exactly who he was, although the boy she remembered had been shorter than her back then. "You must've hit one doozy of a growth spurt. Don't you dare belch out the alphabet," she said with a laugh, remembering how he'd done that all the time to the amusement of their classmates.

"That was a phase. I'm over it."

"That's good. How are you?"

"Great. Married. Three amazing girls. Not a one of them burps the alphabet, by the way."

"Thank goodness. With a last name like Belcher, I guess you came by it honestly."

"Stopped the teasing. Kind of the 'if you can't beat 'em, join 'em' approach. Worked every time."

He'd been a jokester throughout school. The poor teachers had had their hands full with him. "Three children. And you still live here in Burnt Chimney. I thought you'd become a famous comedian. You were always doing crazy things for a laugh. Or maybe a rock star. Do you still play the guitar?"

"Nope. Found my calling right here in town. I'm a pastor."

"A—?" She swallowed back her surprise. "That's the last thing I would have guessed."

"Being playful doesn't offend Jesus. I know what's important, and Lord knows I see proof of it every day. Real blessings."

She tried to remember the last time she set foot in a church. It must've been when her boss got married. Too long ago.

"Your grandpa Johnny never missed a Sunday."

"That doesn't surprise me." Church was an important part of family life in Burnt Chimney.

"You sure made a mess. There's glass everywhere. Let me help you clean that up. I know where the broom is."

He went into the kitchen and came back and went straight to work.

"I don't mind," he said when she protested. "Better for me to nick one of these rough hands than your delicate ones."

She turned her hands over. "Thank you for doing that."

He lifted the dustpan and started back toward the kitchen.

"Wait!" She rushed over to him and looked in the dustpan. "Thank goodness. The cuff link." She held it between her finger and thumb. "That would've been terrible if we accidentally threw it away."

"It was so special to your grandfather. Sorry. I didn't see it."

"It was very special." How had he not noticed that? She eyed him cautiously, but he had a sincere look of surprise on his face as he apologized.

Reed smiled gently, and she wondered if he was reading her mind. She regretted thinking for even a second that he might have been trying to make off with it.

"We have a wonderful congregation. You're going to love it," Reed said. "I came by to pick up your grandpa's Bible and a couple of pictures to put up to help people remember him as he was. I'm preparing for his service. I hope you don't mind if I take the Bible with me."

"No, of course. I understand. Oh goodness, I haven't seen any pictures. I can look around."

"No need. I know where everything is. He and I shared many a cup of coffee at that table in there. And tea on the front porch."

And all she had was phone calls. Advice about trivial things. They never discussed anything more substantial. She'd been more apt to talk about the weather. The most precious moments in those long phone calls were his poems. He had a new poem to read to her every time they talked. She'd gotten to where she typed them as he read them to her, wanting to hang on to them. She was so glad she had.

"You know, Reed. Or should I call you Pastor Belcher?"

"Reed is fine."

"I have some poetry he wrote for me that I could share with you."

"That would be great." He walked across the room and tugged open the drawer on the side table next to the recliner and retrieved the Bible.

She stared at the worn leather cover, and a lump came to her throat.

"A well-worn Bible is a sign of a well-fed soul." He patted the tattered leather then walked over to the bookcase and grabbed a shoebox from the top shelf. "Pictures. Do you want to look through them first?"

"No. Take them. Whatever you need," Eliana said.

"What is it *you* need, Eliana?"

"Me?" That was a loaded question. "I don't know. I need to know he wasn't in pain. Or afraid. I wish I'd realized. Well, it's just silly, but I never thought about him not being around."

"I hope it's comforting to hear that your grandfather was not afraid." He held up the Bible. "His comfort came from these words. We have a glorious, unparalleled hope as Christians. Hang on to that."

"I will."

"Your grandfather loved to mark his favorite scriptures in here. I'm going to share some of them at his service."

"I would love that. I can email the poems to you, if that's okay."

"Sure." He picked up a notepad from the end table, scribbled on it, and handed it to her. His kind eyes held her gaze. "Your grandfather was very proud of you. He loved sharing your accomplishments with us. You may have not been here in Burnt Chimney, but you were surely in Johnny Turner's life."

"Thank you for sharing that, Reed. It's comforting."

"You call if I can be of help. For anything."

"I will. Thank you."

"I also gave you my phone number." He smiled. "Use it any time, day or night."

Although she was technically Grandpa Johnny's last living relative, she felt quite certain that he was surrounded by many people who were just like family in this town, and she was grateful for that.

Reed walked outside, and that was when Eliana saw why she hadn't heard him drive up. He got on a bicycle and placed the Bible in the wire basket that hung from the handlebars. He flipped the kickstand with his heel. "Sorry I busted in that way and scared you. When I saw the light on, I was afraid some kids might've broken in looking for trouble. I'll see you at the service on Saturday, unless you call sooner." He smiled. "We have Sunday service at ten. We'd love to see you there."

He left, and darkness fell over the little house in the country. She had no memories of how noisy country nights were, but standing there on the front porch, it didn't take long for the sounds to chase her inside. Maybe they'd just been so familiar then they didn't seem as scary.

She set the cuff link back on the mantel on the block of wood. It looked sort of silly there without the glass over it, but it was where it belonged. *I should have left it alone.*

She changed into her pajamas and went to bed, but as tired as she was, sleep just wouldn't come. Finally, she got up and walked through the house, turning on lights as she went.

In Grandpa Johnny's bedroom, the bed was undisturbed, hospital corners and all. Granny Mae had once told her that Grandpa was the one who'd taught her to make a bed like that. Her own mother hadn't been a good housekeeper, and he'd taught her just about everything she knew. Eliana was almost twelve when Granny Mae passed. Grandpa Johnny was heartbroken, and it tormented Eliana that her mother took her away from him and Daddy less than a year later with no explanation except that she wasn't happy living there.

She lay across his bed, staring at the ceiling in the darkness. The moon was just a sliver, but finally her eyes began to adjust, and memories of how deep her sadness was when they first left Burnt Chimney came back in a rush.

She wondered what her life would have been like if she'd never left this town.

My life is somewhere else, and there are no do-overs.

Reliving that grief was hard. She got up and turned on the light then walked downstairs.

She pulled the worn blanket from the back of the couch and snuggled against the throw pillow, whispering a quiet prayer before closing her eyes.

∾ CHAPTER SIX ∾

Camron got up with the sun, like he did every day, but this morning he found himself stalling. Instead of carrying his coffee out to check the livestock first thing, he sat at his kitchen table with his elementary school yearbook opened to the picture of Johnny Turner's granddaughter. He took a sip of his coffee and then pushed the mug away as he swallowed the lukewarm liquid.

I've been sitting here way too long.

He shut the book and carried it back to put on the shelf.

In school, Eliana was quiet. Even at recess time she'd read rather than play, but on weekends when the neighbors got together at the Turners' house, she came alive, skipping through the yard and fearlessly swinging higher than anyone else dared.

Camron could still picture the way her hair tumbled across her shoulders when she tossed her head and laughed. He'd convinced himself once that she was a twin. The serious one went to school, and the other resided at Mr. Johnny and Miss Mae's house all day, every day.

He lived for those Sunday afternoons with Eliana when she sparkled like a shooting star. Bright, unexpected, and awesome.

Until that Sunday, with no warning and no explanation, she and her mom were gone. While everyone else was at church, they drove away and never came back. People whispered about it for the longest time, but after another school year went by, it was clear they weren't returning to Burnt Chimney.

Over the years, though, as Camron got to know Johnny Turner better, he learned the whole story. He also discovered where Eliana had gotten her carefree attitude. Johnny Turner was a kid at heart right up to the day he died, and anyone who spent time with the man couldn't help but become a little more like him. Camron appreciated Johnny for that. It was something he missed having with his own father, who had always been so dedicated to his dental practice that they didn't spend much time together.

Camron put his cup in the sink, stuffed a protein bar into his pocket for later, and left the house.

He loved spring mornings like this one, where the dew was light, the sky clear blue, and the melody from the birds whistling with delight made everything else seem a million miles away. He got in the farm utility vehicle and started the engine.

Just then Reed coasted to a stop on his bicycle right next to him.

"Hey, Reed," Camron greeted him. "You're up early."

"On a beautiful day like this I don't waste a single moment. I wanted to stop in and see how're you holding up. I know how close you and Johnny were."

Just the mention of Johnny's name made Camron hitch a breath. "Johnny was more of a dad to me than my own for most of my life. You know that better than anyone." Camron shut down the UTV.

"For the most part, parents do the best they can," Reed said. "Nobody ever said they were perfect."

This wasn't the first time he'd had this particular talk with Reed. It was unfortunate Camron's father could only be happy if

Camron followed in his footsteps, but Camron didn't want to be stuck in an office. He preferred to roll up his sleeves and work the land, something his father would never understand. "I still can't believe he's gone."

"The man was ninety-three years old. His death isn't a complete shock. These bodies were never built to last indefinitely."

"I'm not even forty, and I have more aches and pains than Johnny ever complained about."

"You'll carry on the things he taught you to the next generation," Reed said. "He was a good man, wasn't he? Always one of the first to volunteer to help no matter what we needed."

"And boy, wouldn't it have been nice if he *hadn't* helped on pancake supper nights," Camron joked.

If there was one thing Johnny Turner wasn't good at, it was making pancakes. He made the heaviest, toughest flapjacks ever. Light and fluffy must not be how they made them in the army. People could barely get them down without multiple refills of milk or coffee, and that about broke the bank. It was a long-running joke among the members of the men's group that they lost money on pancake supper night if Johnny made the pancakes.

Truth was, there'd been so much bellyaching about his pancakes from the congregation, they'd had to trick Johnny out of cooking for a while. When that failed, they'd monitored his every step until they figured out the problem was that he wasn't letting the batter rest.

So from then on, whenever Johnny cooked on pancake night, Reed would have Camron lure Johnny out of the kitchen on some bogus task so the batter rested and the gluten had time to relax.

After that, the pancakes turned out perfectly, and Camron was pretty sure Johnny was never the wiser.

"We missed you Monday night. The pancakes were perfect," Reed said with a laugh.

Camron shouldn't have been surprised they made it a pancake supper night in honor of Johnny. "I was dressed and ready to go, but when I got into my car, I turned right to pick up Johnny like always. When it clicked that he was no longer here… I just couldn't do it. I sat on his porch until after dark that night."

"I thought it might have been something like that." Reed leaned forward and settled his forearms on the handlebars. "It's okay. There will be hard days for us, for this whole town, for that matter, but Johnny's in the most glorious place of all."

"I know that."

"Take all the time you need, Camron. You can trust He has a plan, and it's perfect."

"I'm a better man because of Johnny."

"I'm pretty sure you were always going to be a good man."

"Can we talk about something else?" Camron's chest tightened.

"Sure. I just wanted to check on you. Actually, that's not entirely true. There is one more thing."

Camron braced himself, praying Reed wasn't getting ready to ask him to speak at the funeral. Camron couldn't imagine doing that. This grief thing was real, and he was having trouble just getting through his chores and remembering to take another breath, it ached in his chest so deeply.

Reed said, "I was headed to the church last night, and when I passed by Johnny's place, I saw lights on. I was afraid a couple of those boys, you know who I'm talking about, might be getting into trouble over there, knowing Johnny wasn't around. Anyway, I stopped in to check to make sure things were okay, and you won't believe who I found."

"Eliana."

"So, you already know? She's back in town. Still single too. Were you surprised to see her?"

"A little. Eliana and Johnny were close, but she lives on the other side of the country."

"She looks good."

"She does." He'd be lying if he argued, but he knew what Reed was thinking.

Reed smiled. "You used to pine away for that girl. Now that you're both all grown up, I can imagine it would be nice for the two of you to catch up. Maybe…"

"That was a long time ago. We—"

Reed raised his hand. "Mmhmm. Okay, well, I didn't know if you knew she was in town, so I figured I'd pass on the 411 and let nature take its course."

"The only nature taking its course was in the flower beds. She'd just gotten to the house when I went by to water the flowers and caught her by surprise."

"I surprised her too," Reed said.

Camron wondered if Reed had been greeted by a flurry of pine cones to the head and chest too.

"How long is she here for?" Reed asked.

"I don't know. At least until after the funeral."

"Maybe you could persuade her to stay a little longer."

"I've got a fence to tend to. Did you need anything else?"

"Not a thing. I hope I'll see you at the service this weekend."

"Yeah. I'll be there. And I'll be at the next men's ministry meeting too." The work would go on, if not as smoothly, being short a man like Johnny.

Camron watched as Reed pedaled back down the path toward the road.

Just then, getting through the funeral was the real hurdle.

✑ Chapter Seven ✑

Eliana's alarm went off at nine, and it was a good thing she'd set it because even though she was an early bird by design, three time zones took some getting used to.

Best to get on the time zone you're in and roll with it. Her boss had given her that advice when she first started traveling for the company, and it had served her well.

She groaned and sat up. She'd much rather roll over and go back to sleep, but she really wanted to get this visit over and done with and not have to stay into next week.

All she could hope for was that she would find Nelson Luther sitting at his desk, sipping coffee and waiting for her with all the necessary paperwork.

Just the thought of him drinking coffee made her eager to have some herself.

She hopped out of bed and made a pot then carried a full cup with her as she curled up on the corner of the sofa. Sunlight streamed into the room.

She missed Grandpa Johnny clanking around cast-iron pans and whistling from the kitchen.

She took comfort in the rustle of activity outside. A squirrel was giving birds at the feeder a hearty dose of advice, which the birds seemed to find amusing. Bees tickled the centers of the brilliant pink azaleas along the front porch, and a pair of cardinals skittered from the forsythia to the dogwood tree.

Eliana took in a long, slow breath, trying to interrupt the lonely moment with gratitude for all the memories and love she felt sitting here surrounded by Grandpa Johnny's things.

To hear Mom talk, every minute living in Burnt Chimney had been torture.

After a while, Eliana had believed her, but as she got older and saw the trail of bitterness Mom left in her wake, she separated her personal experience from what her mother had drilled into her head.

It was a good thing she'd been able to do that. She'd always known Grandpa Johnny and Granny Mae were good people, and she needed desperately to know that her father had loved her.

Her initial contact was met with such joy and positive emotion that it was easy for her to open her heart and have a relationship with Dad and Grandpa Johnny again, even though she kept it from her mom to keep the peace.

She only had a couple of chances with her dad before he died, but those visits had filled her with something she'd been aching for. Unconditional love and understanding. Losing him so soon after reuniting had been devastating, and Grandpa Johnny was the only one who understood that. Not being able to talk about it with Mom had made it harder.

Now, losing Grandpa Johnny reopened those wounds.

If only I'd visited Grandpa Johnny more often after Dad died.

Here I am in my midthirties. Never married. No family left. Just a job that's less fulfilling than it was in the beginning. An apartment I barely spend time in and no real friends outside of work.

What have I done?

Feeling empty and alone, she prayed silently for guidance.

Then she opened her eyes and tipped her chin toward heaven. "God, I know it's been a while, and I've been shortsighted. Please help me see Your plan. Guide me."

She sat there for a long time. Crying. Listening. Wondering. And then it was as if strength washed over her. She swept away the remnants of her tears.

"Whatever happens today, I'm trusting it will all become clear in Your time."

And with those simple words, she felt empowered by the promise that it would be okay. Whether Nelson Luther had everything prepared wouldn't be a problem. So what if she had to slow down and give this time for Grandpa Johnny? Didn't he at least deserve that? He'd been so good to her.

She got dressed then tucked a notebook and pen in her handbag to take with her. With the address typed into her GPS, she set out on the drive to Rocky Mount.

The main crossroads in Burnt Chimney still had the same little service station she remembered, but straight across the street there was one of those sprawling gas stations with a drive-through convenience store. She wondered how long the mom-and-pop service station on the corner would survive that.

It didn't take long to get to Rocky Mount. She pulled into an empty parking spot along the curb in front of an old brick two-story building just down from the courthouse.

NELSON LUTHER, ATTORNEY-AT-LAW glistened in gold letters on the glass panel of the door. She gripped the antique brass door handle and stepped inside.

A young woman sat behind an enormous desk in the reception area. She raised her head and smiled at Eliana.

"Good morning. I'm Eliana Tur—"

The woman jumped to her feet. "You're Johnny Turner's granddaughter! It is *so* nice to meet you. Mr. Turner was the nicest man. He was like a great-granddaddy to everyone around here. Especially me. Mama said she and you used to hang out at his house together."

"Hello. Oh, goodness." Eliana tried to process the information. "Who is your mother?"

"Penny Wagner." The young woman grinned, and Eliana caught the similarities of their smiles. "I'm Christina."

"Penny's daughter?" Eliana was overwhelmed with emotion as she did the math in her head. This young woman could practically be her own daughter. "Your mom and I were best friends. She was a little older than me. It was like having a big sister. We spent so much time together at Grandpa Johnny's."

"That's what she said. Wow," Christina gushed. "It's so nice to finally meet you."

"The last summer I lived in Burnt Chimney, your mother and I buried a time capsule under the bridge by the creek. I wonder if she remembers that?"

"A time capsule? I don't remember her ever mentioning it. Did you dig it up?"

"No. We said we'd open it together when I turned forty. Which seemed ancient back then. Doesn't sound so far away now. I can't wait to catch up with her."

The young lady glanced down. "Momma passed almost eight years ago now."

Eliana's eyes filled with tears. "I didn't know." Had Grandpa Johnny told her? She couldn't remember, but if he had, just how busy had she been that she wouldn't remember a thing like that? Eliana reached for Christina's hand. "I am sorry. I bet she was a wonderful mother."

"The best. We were so close," said Christina. "Sorry to have to tell you that. I mean, I know you must be heartbroken about Johnny too."

"Yes. No, it's fine. You were so young when she passed. I'm sorry. Please let me know if there's anything I can do for you."

"It would be fun to hear about when you were friends."

"I'd love to share those memories with you."

Christina pressed on. "When I was saving money for college, your grandfather hired me to work the gardens around his house. Virginia Tech is expensive, even with my scholarship. Anyway, he told me about how you used to dream of having a cut flower farm."

"I haven't thought about the cut flowers in years." Not since she'd left Burnt Chimney. "It feels like a lifetime ago."

"I learned so much working with him. He's the smartest man I ever knew. Lots of people say that about him."

"I agree." Eliana's heart lifted.

"I graduated from Tech and started my own landscaping company on the other side of Wirtz. My aunt is Mr. Luther's secretary. She needed some time off, and so I told her I'd fill in."

"You're already a business owner. That's impressive."

"Your grandfather said I reminded him of you. I always thought that was a huge compliment. He said you're really successful." Christina caught herself. "I'm sorry. I guess all the time with my plants makes me talk too much. Can I help you with something?"

"Yes. I have an appointment this morning with Mr. Luther about my grandfather's estate."

Christina blanched. "I'm sorry. He got called away unexpectedly. I take it no one called you?"

Eliana shook her head. "Do you know how long he'll be?"

"I don't. Sorry. He's been handling his own schedule with my aunt being out. I just assumed he would've called you himself. She asked me to cover the desk for the day. I expect he'll be back on Monday."

There was no sense in complaining about him not letting her know, but boy, did it irritate her. She sucked in a deep breath. "Can you put me on his calendar for first thing Monday morning, please?"

"Well, let me see. I used to know how to use the scheduler program. I helped out on my breaks sometimes." She tapped the keyboard. "Yes. Yes, I can. How about nine forty-five? He'll be done with his first appointment by nine thirty."

"Thank you. I appreciate that." She turned to leave and then turned back. "If you get word he won't be here Monday, would you mind letting me know?"

"I can do that. Let me see if your phone number is in the system." She did some more tapping. "Yep. Got it right here. I'll be sure to text or call you if there's any issue with Monday."

Eliana headed for the door, but then something stopped her. She slowly turned. "Christina, let's get together. I want to hear about your mom and your work with Grandpa Johnny."

"I'd love that so much." Christina grabbed a tissue and dabbed her eyes. "You don't know how much that would mean to me."

I think I do. "Good. You've got my number. Let me know when you'd like to come by."

"I will. Thank you so much." Christina let out a breath. "I can't wait."

CHAPTER EIGHT

Eliana walked out of the lawyer's office knowing she had no choice now but to stay in Burnt Chimney through the weekend at the very least.

And where that would have bothered her before, she found herself to be perfectly okay with it now.

Once Nelson Luther finally got back to town, putting the house on the market should be a quick and easy process since it was in such great shape. He'd already said the house was all but hers. It sounded like just a matter of paperwork, so she might as well enjoy herself.

In no hurry now, she walked down the block. There were some cute storefronts on this path. A coffee shop that boasted the best bear claws in three counties next to a cake bakery. She went into the Bee Hive, a shop with beautiful wooden breakfront cabinets filled with products containing honey. There was everything from lip balm to flavored honey and even fun bee-themed gifts. There was also a beautiful display of fine teas.

She picked out a sweet, fruity black tea with hints of vanilla and caramel, and a box of flavored honey straws. She couldn't wait to sit on the front porch with a cup of tea and try out the different flavors of honey that came in not only clover, lemon, and orange but also mint chocolate and raspberry. As she walked through the store toward the register, she stopped in front of some dish towels with fun little sayings on them displayed on an old ladder painted blue. One caught her eye, and she picked it up. *Faith Can Move Mountains* was written in crisp black letters over a watercolor reflection of mountains that looked almost like the view from Grandpa Johnny's house.

"Isn't that lovely?" The store clerk walked over. "I've got a gift box for it."

"I love it, but I won't need a box. It's for me."

"Even better. Can I take those to the counter for you while you browse?"

Eliana relinquished her findings with a thank-you and continued to look around.

"Are you needing anything in particular?"

"No ma'am. Just kind of wandering around today."

"Take your time. There are a couple of other new shops on the next block, and two nice antique stores that have been here forever. If you're sticking around for lunch, Ippy's has wonderful salads and burgers. I love their Lumberjack sandwich."

"I never realized there were so many cute places to visit in this town."

"It's a wonderful place to live. You must be passing through."

Eliana wasn't sure how to answer that. "Well, sort of. I went to elementary school in Burnt Chimney. My grandfather just passed away. I'm here for the funeral and a short visit to settle the estate."

"I'm sorry for your loss. You should really think about staying longer. I have no doubt being back after so long will feel like a warm hug. People around here are like that."

"Thank you." Eliana paid for her things and left. Her phone chimed. Christina texted that Nelson would return to the office on Monday, but he needed to move their appointment to Tuesday at nine forty-five.

THAT'S FINE. I'LL SEE HIM THEN.

If she was going to be forced into vacation time, this wouldn't have been her destination of choice, but it could be worse.

From her car, she called the airline to cancel her return flight that had been scheduled for six o'clock Sunday morning. She'd rebook when things got straightened out at the beginning of the week. Good thing Nelson had purchased a fully refundable ticket. She wouldn't even have to pay a change fee.

Now, other than the funeral, she'd have at least five days with no plans. Maybe longer.

I shouldn't waste one day of it. She got out of her car. Spending the day here in Rocky Mount was a decent start. For a second, she considered going back to the house and making a lazy day out of it, stretching out like a cat in a sunny spot on the porch.

Then again, lazy never was her style.

She stashed her sweater in the car so the warm sun could kiss her skin as she walked.

A sandwich board propped in front of the antique store boasted a 10-percent-off sale in bright green and purple chalk. In orange, they'd scrawled the words Now Serving Free Coffee in big letters across the bottom.

Coffee sounds good.

She went inside where indeed there was a lovely coffee bar just to the right of the front door on an old metal Hoosier cabinet. Mugs in festive colors lined the counter next to the coffeepot and a spinner full of assorted flavored tea and coffee pods. She fixed herself a cup and then began browsing through the store.

A young woman approached her. "Good morning! I'm Mitzy. Let me know if I can help you with anything."

"I will," Eliana said. "Thanks for the coffee."

"You're welcome. It was my idea. Dad thought it was crazy, but it's pulled a lot more people in off the street this week. I think the return on investment for what it cost me to set it up is already proving me right."

"Who's talking about me?" A man popped around the corner, wagging his finger. "I hear you," he said with a chuckle. "Family business," he explained to Eliana.

"She's onto something, sir," Eliana said. "I wasn't planning to stop in here this morning, but I couldn't pass up the coffee."

"Excellent. Now sip it slow enough that you can't pass up some other little treasure while you're in here." The elderly man turned to his daughter. "That's where the profit gets calculated."

"I'll see what I can do to help you out there, Mitzy. I think it's a great idea." Eliana took a sip of her coffee. It was a quaint shop. Hints of vanilla and something woodsy hung in the air. *Probably years of dust too*, she thought as she picked up a leather-bound novel sitting on a marble-top end table and opened it to the copyright page. Not a first edition. She placed it back on the table and wandered down the long row of glass cases filled with jewelry and collectibles.

Most of it looked to be estate jewelry. She didn't have an eye for whether it was real or fake, but some of it was quite pretty. She was drawn to a blue velvet display holding nearly a dozen necklaces.

Something about the lovely engraving on them caught her eye. A handwritten tag noted they were from the early 1900s.

"You like those?" Mitzy was already jiggling through a hoop of keys.

"Eye-catching. They have heirloom quality. There must be a story behind them."

"I'm sure there is, but I don't have the details on but two of them that we bought from estate sales here in the area. My dad is nuts over these things. He's always scouting around for them. Honestly, I'm not sure he actually wants to sell any of them. But I, on the other hand, will sell them in a heartbeat. Most of the pendants were crafted out of silver coins." She set the velvet tray on the counter. "We have a few made from gold coins."

"Coins? I thought we weren't supposed to deface currency."

Mitzy laughed. "If I had a nickel for every time I heard that. Think about it. Those tourist-attraction penny-stretcher machines would be outlawed if altering coins was illegal. You can't go changing a coin to pass it off as something it's not. Like taking a leg off one of those buffalo nickels to make it look like a rare coin. That would be fraud, but this is perfectly legal. There are also several beautiful pieces of coin jewelry at the Smithsonian Institute. Ever been there?"

"I haven't." If Eliana had lived in Burnt Chimney for two more years, she'd have been able to go to the Smithsonian on the annual high school field trip. She'd always thought the nation's capital would be an interesting place to visit with all its history. *I might need to put that on my bucket list.* Eliana had never thought about traveling for fun, but after losing Johnny she suddenly felt that making some of those things a priority would be a good idea and probably make him happy that she finally took his advice.

Mitzy's dad walked over. "Each one is unique, but if you know what to look for, you can tell by the craftsmanship the same jeweler made them." He pulled a loupe from his shirt pocket and raised it to his eye, peering closer at a particularly lovely pendant. "Yes, see up in the right corner, the jeweler etched a little symbol." He handed her the loupe.

Eliana lifted it to her eye and leaned forward. "What does it say?"

"Tutz. It's short for Tutzauer."

"I do see it," she marveled.

"He was known for making love tokens in this region. The prettiest ones, if you ask me."

"Love tokens?" She reached for a smaller one. Her favorite of the bunch. "My grandmother used to wear something like this one."

"That's an especially nice one. There's an inscription on the back of it," he said, removing it from the display and holding it out to her. "Look through the loupe."

She raised the shiny charm close to her face.

"Love tokens were very popular in the 1800s," he explained, "and even around both World Wars. Most of them carried a monogram, and some had special dates."

"So how do you know these are love tokens?"

"There are two giveaways. First, they have to be made from a real coin and smoothed on at least one side. Secondly, the engraving has to have been done by hand."

"I can't believe I've never heard of this before."

"Although often the love tokens have triple overlapping initials, like a typical modern monogram, it's been said that some men would have the love token monogrammed with the woman's first initial and his own surname initial as a proposal asking her to take his name."

"That's so romantic. I love that." She looked at the coin again. "Tutzauer made this one too. That's cool. I wonder if he made my grandmother's."

"He may have. Was she local?"

"Yes. Mae Turner."

The man relaxed his posture, pressing his hands on the shiny smudge-free glass. "You're Johnny Turner's granddaughter?"

"I am."

"I'm so sorry for your loss," he said. "It's nice to meet you, and I can tell you it's a very good chance that the one Johnny had made for Mae was made by Tutz. You can borrow the loupe to look if you like. Take it with you and drop it back by another day."

"Thank you, but that's not necessary." She held up her phone. "I'll take a picture and blow it up. Half the things on labels these days are printed so small, I've become quite the expert."

"Technology. Of course you can. Well, it's very nice to meet you. Take your time. If there's anything I can show you, just yell. I'd be happy to help."

"Thank you. I definitely will. There's so much to see." She turned around and was startled to see Camron standing behind her, smiling. People were popping up all over the place in this shop.

"Fancy meeting you here," he said.

"And you. What are you doing in an antique shop in the middle of the morning?" she asked.

"Delivering fresh hamburger to Mr. Pritchard here." Camron nodded to the cooler on the cart behind him.

"Do I need to remind you that you run a dairy farm?" she teased. "Got milk? And all that?"

He groaned and shook his head. "Not the first time I've heard that. I'm here to tell you that even dairy animals make great hamburger, Eliana."

"They sure do," the store owner said. "I've been expecting you, Camron." Mr. Pritchard came around the counter. "I can take that to the freezer." He swept the handle from Camron and darted toward the rear of the store. "I'll bring your check. Give me a minute."

He and the cart disappeared between a stack of hatboxes and a cannon replica.

"Are you in town for some shopping?" Camron asked.

"No. I was supposed to meet with Grandpa Johnny's lawyer this morning, but I guess he got called away. Some family emergency or something," she said.

"Well, it looks like you found a good way to spend your time. They have some great stuff in here." He glanced over her shoulder. "I saw Mr. Pritchard showing you the love tokens. You like those?"

She raised an eyebrow in doubt. "What do you know about jewelry from the early 1900s?"

"Pretty much everything your grandpa told me about them. I never fact-checked it myself, but he's a pretty credible source. He gave your grandmother one because his dad had given his mom one when he fell in love with her."

"I remember her wearing that necklace," she said. "I never asked her about it."

"You know how much Johnny loved traditions."

"That's true, but love tokens? How does that just come up in casual conversation?"

"It didn't. He had the one your grandmother used to wear hanging on a nail next to the sink. I asked him about it one day. He said his mother had told him about them and how special hers was to her. It's how he asked Mae to marry him."

"I can't believe I never knew that," she said. "It's the most romantic thing I've ever heard."

"I still recall the look in his eyes when he told me about it. It was a special memory for him too. I expect you'll find your grandmother's and maybe even great-grandmother's necklaces when you go through Johnny's things. I'm sure he would have kept them somewhere special."

Mr. Pritchard approached, carrying a check. "Here you go, Camron. Thanks for delivering it."

"Happy to do it." Camron turned back to Eliana. "I'll see you around."

"Yeah. Actually, I was wondering... Do you think we could talk about the house? I have some questions. I figure since you did so much of the work, you'd be able to help me."

"Sure. When?"

"Tomorrow?"

"Sounds good. I'll come by after chores in the morning. Does that work for your schedule?"

"My calendar is emptier than it's been in longer than I can remember," Eliana told him.

His chin lifted. "Don't know what to do with yourself, do you?"

"I honestly do not." She wasn't sure if that was a good or a bad thing.

❦ CHAPTER NINE ❧

The next morning Camron fed the cows then checked the herd that grazed Johnny's pasture on the back side. He drove down the hill and over the bridge that connected the two properties. He and Johnny used this shortcut more often than not.

He pulled the truck through the paddock and got out. He clapped his hands twice and whistled through his teeth. The third-trimester heifers he'd moved to this pasture lumbered his way.

All were accounted for, so he tossed a couple of bales of fresh hay into the rack then topped off the minerals and poured scoops of feed into the trough. While they ate, he touched each cow, checking for signs indicating calving was soon. All seemed to be going to plan.

He got back in his truck. A cow let out a long, moaning moo.

"I hear you," he said. Funny how some of them were more vocal than others when they wanted attention. "I'll come see you again later."

Satisfied everyone was doing fine, he drove to the next gate. The warm weather was rewarding him with beautiful pastures, and the field that Johnny had him plant for the bees was dotted with bright pink bee balm, purple coneflowers, and wild blue and white false indigo flowers that already stretched over three feet tall. The four rows of lavender he'd insisted on had come up so nice this year, the fourth since they'd planted it and the strongest stand they'd had so far.

He'd have to find someone from the apiary club to come tend to Johnny's beehives. It wasn't something Camron had ever taken the time to learn. He pulled his knife from its sheath on his belt and cut a handful of purple coneflowers and bee balm flowers that looked like hot-pink cheerleader pom-poms. He carried them back to the truck and cut a piece of orange baling twine to tie the stems together with a passable shoelace bow.

When he drove up to Johnny's, he wasn't even halfway to the porch before Eliana bounced out the front door. The way the morning sun caught her hair made it seem to glitter like gold.

"Hey there." Her smile faded when she spotted the makeshift bouquet. "You brought me flowers?"

"Not exactly." He shoved them toward her awkwardly. "They're Johnny's flowers. Technically, yours?"

She accepted them, dipping her face into them and inhaling deeply. "What does that mean?"

"That I'm giving you your own flowers, I suppose. They're growing on the back forty. He had me plant flowers for the pollinators. You know the—"

"Yes, I'm aware of what pollinators are. Birds, butterflies, bees."

"Good, because Johnny has some fancy eight-frame beehives that are going to need tending. Bees are not my forte. It's hard to herd critters that fly and won't come to a feed bucket."

Eliana laughed. "I'm picturing you with a little bee lasso."

"Real funny." He shot her a less than amused look.

"It is."

He relaxed into a grin. "Okay, so it is. That being said. Do you know anything about bees?"

"Not much call for that in my line of business."

"Too bad."

"I made something for us to eat." She looked pleased.

He hadn't expected that. "Really? Wait a minute. Do you mean to tell me that I didn't impress you with my sandwich-making skills?"

"No. Quite the opposite. You impressed me so much I felt like I needed to step up to keep up." She turned, gesturing him to follow her inside. "Come on in."

"Good, because I'm hungry. Bring it on." He followed her into the kitchen, where it looked like she had everything prepared to cook. She twisted the knob on the gas range, sending the flame flickering below a cast-iron skillet, then did pirouetted to the sink, where she filled a small pitcher with water and put the flowers into it.

He leaned over the stove. "What are you making?"

"Well, I have to use what I have here, and it just so happens I have everything on hand to make one of Grandpa's favorites. Well, it used to be when I was a kid. Grilled peanut butter, apple, and honey sandwiches."

"I hope you can make them as well as Johnny did. Because he made them for me too, and I love them."

"I pretty much mastered the art before I was ten. I think I've got this."

The stacked sandwiches sizzled as soon as they hit the cast iron. She stood patiently with the spatula in her hand, giving them time for the bread to crisp up, then turned them over. Not one apple slice slipped out. Even Johnny had flubbed that now and again. "You get extra points for style."

Eliana exaggerated a bow. "I'm glad you approve." She plated the sandwiches and handed one of them to Camron. "Want to eat outside?"

"Too pretty a day to be cooped up. Lead the way." He followed her to the porch, where she already had a pitcher of sweet tea sitting on the table next to a big metal mixing bowl filled with ice.

"Thank you for this," Camron said. "I had no idea I was going to get the royal treatment."

"Well, you did bring me flowers."

"From your own yard."

"Still a nice gesture."

"You're welcome." He took a bite of his sandwich. "Perfect." From the expression on her face, it was clear she was pleased with the compliment. And that made him happy too.

They ate without any more banter, and that was kind of nice. He poured himself a glass of tea. "How are you doing? Are you settling in?"

"Yes. I've got everything I need." She shrugged. "I'm sad, but it's nice here. So much quieter than I remembered, but then, I was probably the source of the noise in those days."

"You, me, Penny, Reed, the others. Yeah, it was fun to hang out here when we were kids."

"I think I kind of like it quiet. I must be getting old."

"No, we're not getting old. We're just appreciating different things. When I went to college, I missed this place like crazy. The air breathes cleaner, don't you think?"

"That's true."

"Did you happen to see how dark the sky was last night?"

Eliana shook her head. "I was so tired."

"It looked like you could grab handfuls of stars. I don't think I got a good night's sleep the whole time I was in college."

"That must've made you cranky."

"I think what made me cranky was that I was following Dad's dream. I got my bachelor's in business and was supposed to head to dental school, you know, become a partner in his practice, but I came home that summer, and while helping my grandfather I realized the dairy farm was what made me happy. My dad wasn't too keen about it, but I had to follow my heart."

"I bet your grandfather was thrilled."

"He was. I think it would've killed him if the hard work he'd put in all those years would die with him."

"That would've been terrible."

"I wish Dad saw it that way. In the end, I had to do what was going to be right for me for the rest of my life, and I knew it wasn't following in my father's footsteps. I've learned to live with his disappointment."

"I know that had to be a hard decision to make."

"It wasn't an easy decision to disappoint him, but I'm proud of all I've accomplished."

"How are your parents? Your dad is still a dentist, right?"

"Yes, and he's still working too many hours and complaining about it. I get together with them for dinner sometimes, but it's been a little tough on our relationship. He's prickly. Mom's dying to do some traveling. She wants to go on a church mission trip, and Dad keeps saying 'next year.' I think she's afraid next year will never come."

"That doesn't sound great, but having lost both Mom and Dad, and now Grandpa Johnny, even a complaining family sounds pretty awesome." She took in a deep breath and turned to him. "I wanted to ask you. Did you know I liked you when we were kids?"

"I wish I had. You were my best friend, and I had the biggest crush on you."

"You did?"

"I didn't want to lose your friendship by telling you. Actually, it was probably more that I was just afraid to."

"So?" She raised her shoulders nearly to her ears. "Why didn't you write me back?"

"You wrote me?"

"I did. Several letters to you, Penny, and Grandpa Johnny. He said he never got them. Did you not get the letters from me either?"

"I didn't." He leaned forward. "I wish I had. You have no idea how sad I was when you left."

"It was a hard time for me too."

"I'm glad you're here now."

She looked a little panicked, taking a long sip of her tea, maybe avoiding a response.

"You did a great job on the upgrades to the house," she finally said. "It's really beautiful."

"Thanks. It was Johnny's vision. I suggested some updated colors, but he made the choices from the paint chips."

"On the flight here, I was making a mental list of the things that would need to be done to sell the place. Aside from upgrading the central air to something a little more energy efficient, this place is ready for the market."

"You'd sell?" If it was his decision, he'd never sell.

"I… Well, I don't live here. Why wouldn't I?"

What do I say that's not going to come across as judgmental? "It's a great place. A part of your past. You could hang on to it for a while. It *has* been in your family for well over a hundred and fifty years."

"True," she said, with only a momentary hesitation. "But I'm not landlord material, and I wouldn't know the first thing about taking care of a place like this. Especially from across the country."

"The neighbors around here are great. They'd help you figure it out." He turned to face her. "I'd be here for you too."

"That's nice of you, but I have a career. And you have a huge farm to manage."

"According to Johnny, that career of yours keeps you on the road most of the time. Does it really matter where you live?"

She opened her mouth but then closed it and blinked. "No, I guess not. It's not something that's ever crossed my mind."

"Well, I'm just saying you have options. You don't have to sell this house. Even if you used it as a getaway a couple times a year, that might be nice."

"I hadn't thought of that."

"Unless you need the money. I guess that would be different."

"No. It's not that." She frowned. "It would make more sense if Grandpa Johnny was still here."

"It makes sense to hang on to the family legacy. Maybe pass it down to your children. Do you want children?"

"I do. I mean I have to get married and all, but there's nothing more I'd like than to have a family."

He pushed his hands into his pockets. She needed to fall in love with this town. He'd only had her back for a couple of days, but he wanted her to stay. "I thought you liked growing up in Burnt Chimney?"

"I did." She shrugged. "Well, I did until Mom packed us up and never looked back."

"It seemed so sudden. You didn't know that was in the works?"

"I had no idea. I even had a birthday sleepover planned with Penny the following weekend. I didn't get to say goodbye to anyone."

"That had to be hard."

"It was."

"Well, don't let what your mom did or said jade your view of Burnt Chimney. Granted, it's small, but it's a good place to live. It's safe, quiet, and…look around. It's beautiful."

"It is that." She tucked a strand of hair behind her ear.

"I guess with all your travel, it might not be too impressive."

"You'd be surprised. All I see of the towns where I'm opening stores is the inside of malls and strip-mall parking lots. And sleeping in hotels is not nearly as glamourous as it sounds."

"So basically, you travel all the time and never experience the places?"

"Right. I told myself I was going to do a better job of tacking on a few days at the end of trips to play tourist, but frankly, I'm so tired when we're done, all I want is to get home and forget about it."

"That's too bad. I haven't done much traveling either, but I'd like to. Places like Pike's Peak in Colorado, turquoise waters in the Caribbean, and this will probably sound crazy, but I'd love to see the whales off the coast of Cabo."

"That doesn't sound crazy at all."

Camron tugged on his ball cap. "I know we just ate lunch, but I was wondering if I could talk you into having dinner with me?" He laughed at the surprised look on her face. "I can show you my operation and all the things Johnny helped me with. It won't be fancy, but I think you'll like it."

"If you're basing the menu off of my eighth-grade palate, then I guess you'll be making me another peanut butter sandwich, this one with jelly instead of apples and honey."

"*Strawberry* jelly. Oh, and a bowl of frosting for dessert."

"You remember that?"

"I do. How about this? I promise I won't serve you anything between two slices of bread, although lunch was delicious. Will you come? I'll even build a fire so we can toast marshmallows. The stars are supposed to be amazing tonight."

She sucked in a breath, and for a minute he thought she was going to decline. "It's not like I have any other plans. Yeah, I'm in."

"You won't regret it." He handed her his phone. "Put your number in. I'll send you the address. It's just on the other side of the hill."

She tapped in her number and handed the phone back to him. "Can I bring something?"

"Not a thing." He tucked the phone into his pocket. "I'll see you tonight."

⌒ Chapter Ten ⌒

Eliana waved to Camron as he pulled out of the driveway.

He'd been so disturbed that she'd consider selling, and frankly, that surprised her. Because there hadn't seemed to be any other feasible option. None that she could see until he listed them off with ease.

She went back inside and used her phone to get a list of Realtors in the area. She figured she might as well get someone to start looking at comps for a ballpark idea of the value of the property. When she had all the data, she could make a good financial decision.

Of course, value wasn't always monetary. She knew that.

She called the office and left a message for her boss, following it up with an email formally requesting additional days off. She had more than three weeks of vacation still on the books from last year and nothing pressing on her schedule. If there was ever a time to burn some vacation, it was probably now.

If she was going to sell, this might be the last opportunity she'd ever have to be back in Burnt Chimney. She looked around at the familiar things. It was comforting to be in this house, in a place where family meant something, and even though her mom and dad had rarely been in sync, she'd felt loved here.

Why was it so hard to ask for time off? I earned it.

That little voice in her head rattled off without hesitation, *Because you're a workaholic.*

Or maybe that was Grandpa Johnny's voice she heard. He'd said it plenty of times over the years.

"I won't be working while I'm here, Grandpa. I'm going to leave my laptop in its case and actually take time off."

She grabbed her keys and walked out the door. If she was going to Camron's house tonight, she should at least take a hostess gift or something.

She drove back to Rocky Mount to find something, considering maybe picking up a pretty dessert, but he'd promised her frosting, and as funny as that was, she did still love the frosting more than the cake. She'd be happy if he simply opened a can of it and handed her a spoon.

A cherry on top might be extra nice.

At the grocery store, she stocked up on a few basics to get her through the next week. Almond milk, yogurt, salmon, salad fixings, and a loaf of bread.

She came to a full stop by the rack of Virginia-branded items. She grabbed a dish towel with the famous VIRGINIA IS FOR LOVERS saying on it and then put it back when she saw a flour-sack towel that read MAKE YOURSELF AT HOME, CLEAN MY KITCHEN with an outline of the state of Virginia around the words. Seemed like a win-win. A laugh and an offer to clean, since he cooked.

Happy with the hostess-gift solution, she made her purchases and, on her way out by the exit doors, picked up copies of the free local real estate magazines. She stopped at a gift store up the road and bought a large vase. One big enough for the tall flowers Camron had cut for her earlier. She looked forward to arranging those incredible blossoms in something prettier than a pitcher.

It had been a long time since she'd thought about her childhood dream of making a living by growing flowers on Grandpa Johnny's farm. She'd mused about providing fresh-cut flowers to all the restaurants in the whole state and imagined brides coming to her for the prettiest bouquets in the region, which was comical to think about now, because although she'd always had a green thumb at Grandpa Johnny's side, she'd seen bridal bouquets in a magazine only once. They were probably a lot harder to make than they looked.

I once had a head full of fairy-tale dreams. What happened to them?

She still loved flowers. That hadn't changed. For each grand opening she managed, she would find a local flower market and personally put together an arrangement for the store. It was her gift to the team for their hard work. It was so satisfying to see the arrangement come together like a piece of art. There weren't many satisfying parts of her job anymore.

It was decent work, and very black and white, something she'd needed following the mess of living with her mother's moods, which always seemed to be an ugly shade of gray. Predictable was welcome. Yes or no. Right or wrong. No in between. But that little personal touch, the flowers, was such a wonderful way to finish up each job and a special treat for the people who worked so hard to make it happen under her leadership.

She loved doing that.

If she had enough time, she'd explore the back acreage later and cut some flowers for a special arrangement for Grandpa Johnny's service the next day, even though she'd already placed an order for a lovely funeral spray of white calla lilies, white roses, and teal orchids, which were the closest thing to his favorite color of turquoise.

She thought of Penny's daughter, Christina. How sad that she'd lost her mother at such a young age. Penny had been a good friend.

Penny, I'm sorry I didn't know. I should've been here for your service. I'll bring you flowers too. You have a lovely daughter. I'm so glad to have met her. She looks like you.

Before heading home, she stopped at the hardware store and picked out an inexpensive pair of gardening gloves. The impulse-buy rack by the line at the register held an interesting array of items. Everything from hand cream and lip balm named after chicken droppings to maps and candy. One had a brown, orange, and white wrapper that contained long sticks of chewy vanilla caramel cream candy called Cow Tales. *Okay, so that's probably not the best marketing angle for candy.*

But in that instant, her mind unlocked a memory of weekends battling with them like miniature light sabers and devouring them as she, Reed, Camron, and Penny took turns on the swing at Grandpa Johnny's. Granny Mae always had a crock full of them. Some women decorated the center of their table with flowers, but not Granny Mae. She loved candy, and there was always a bowl of it around. Eliana tossed some Cow Tales into her cart. *Weren't these Camron's favorite when we were kids?*

The elderly woman at the counter rang her up. "Don't ya just love these things?" The clerk flapped one of the candies at her. "I swear I could eat a dozen of them. Did you eat 'em when you were a kid?"

"Yes. I didn't even know they still made them until today."

"Good stuff," the woman said with a smile. "I'll have to get one for my break."

Eliana added one more to her order.

She inserted her debit card, and the woman handed her a little brown bag with the items. Eliana reached in the bag and handed one of the Cow Tales to her. "Here. You have a nice day."

"Well, aren't you the sweetest? Thank you."

"You're welcome." She strolled out of the store, enjoying the impromptu delight she'd shared with the stranger. She could get used to that.

As she got close to her car, she noticed a woman unlocking the door to the real estate office.

"Good morning," Eliana said. "Could you maybe answer a couple of questions about homes in the area, comps, things like that?"

"I sure can." The woman stuck out her hand as she propped her hip between the door and the frame. "Kalli Becker. I know this area like the back of my hand. Come on in."

"Thanks." Eliana followed her into the building. Kalli dropped her handbag on the top of her desk and offered Eliana a seat in one of the cushy leather chairs across from her. "Are you relocating here?"

"Well, technically I am, or was, from around here," Eliana said. "I grew up in Burnt Chimney. We left when I was in grade school."

"Oh my goodness." Kalli scooched back from her desk. "You're Johnny Turner's granddaughter."

Was there anyone in this town who didn't know about her from him? "I am."

"Well, I can't imagine you'd find any better place than your grandfather's. He kept it in tip-top shape. Everyone knows that."

"Yes, it is. I was thinking more about if I sold it."

Kalli's mouth literally dropped open, leaving Eliana feeling almost bad for entertaining the thought of selling. "I mean, you know, in case I decided to—"

"Of course. Yes. Well, it's got one of the prettiest views around. I was just over there for a cookout a few weeks ago. I got the grand tour. He did a bunch of updates last year. Don't know what put the bug in him to do that at his age, but it looks nice."

"What kind of money would a place like that bring?"

"Well, I can easily tell you the tax value." Kalli started clicking on her keyboard. "It's public record, you know."

"I should've thought of that." But she'd never owned a home, so why would she?

"Here it is." Kalli quoted a price that was higher than Eliana expected. "Of course, that doesn't always correlate to an asking price. And in this case there's value in the view, not just the functionality of a place like that. Farming is one thing, and I hate to even say the words out loud, but there's always big money in land development too."

Eliana nodded. She couldn't imagine someone coming in and building streets and gutters and some cookie-cutter houses on the land that her family had owned for over a hundred and fifty years.

"Of course, a lot of the value is in the acreage," Kalli went on. "If you're going to sell, I'd suggest depersonalizing it a bit. You know, make it look like anyone could live there, not an elderly man with fifty-year-old furniture. We're getting lots of younger families wanting to move into the area now that Roanoke is booming. It's not too far a commute for those who want the country life. And the hospital in Roanoke expanded and is bringing new surgeons in all the time. I've sold quite a few estates out this way to those wanting to escape the urban sprawl." She took her hands off her keyboard and leveled a stare at Eliana. "Are you truly considering listing it?"

An hour ago, she would've said yes, but minute-by-minute she was rethinking that. "I don't know. I'll have to make some decisions, so I thought I should at least know what I'm dealing with."

"Yes, you will. Your grandfather was loved, and just about anybody in town will be happy to help you with whatever you need. I know everyone. Call me, and I can connect you with the right people."

"That would be great." Eliana got up to leave.

"Tell you what. I'll pull some comps, just in case, but don't feel obligated to list the house. I don't know what your situation is, but if you haven't thought about living here...please do. I think your grandfather would've loved that."

"I'll keep that in mind." Camron had said people around here helped one another out. He wasn't kidding.

She drove back to Grandpa Johnny's house, remembering how she had walked, hopped, skipped, and even raced school friends down this driveway more times than she could count. It was dusty in the summer heat, so muddy when it rained that it required dodging ankle-deep puddles, and covered with so many leaves in the fall that you could kick them in the air.

But this time of year, the azaleas were in full bloom. A random explosion in no particular pattern of red, white, pinks, and coral overgrew the path. Grandpa Johnny used to say azaleas didn't care how many hours of daylight there were. It was all about the right weather. When the temperature was right and they were happy, they bloomed for weeks.

I hope they bloom all the way to fall for you this year, Grandpa Johnny.

Puffy white clouds raced across the robin's-egg blue sky.

Her phone pinged as she carried the bags inside. After awkwardly freeing her wrists from too many shopping bags, she fumbled it to check the message.

Camron had shared his location with a pin-drop then followed it up with a text.

DON'T USE YOUR GPS. I CAN PICK YOU UP, OR IF YOU USE JOHNNY'S GOLF CART, YOU CAN DRIVE RIGHT UP THE PADDOCK LINE WITHOUT EVEN OPENING A GATE.

She texted back, GRANDPA JOHNNY OWNED A GOLF CART?

IN THE BIG BARN.

10/4. WHAT TIME SHOULD I BE THERE?

HAIR PAST A FRECKLE.

Eliana laughed at the schoolyard joke.

SIX IT IS.

She filled the vase with water, transferred Camron's flowers from the too-small container, and fluffed the stems. A ride on a golf cart sounded like fun, plus she could check out the field of flowers on her way.

She put on a spring dress and sandals, but that was awfully fancy for a dinner with an old friend on a farm.

She tossed the dress aside, changed into khaki pants and a white blouse, and checked herself out in the full-length mirror.

I still look like I'm going to work.

She untucked the shirt and tied the blouse at the waist. A couple of twists of the cuffs gave it a much more casual look. She tugged the belt from the loops of her pants and tossed it back into her suitcase, opting for tennis shoes and gold earrings to dress herself up a bit.

Her makeup took twice as long as it should have. She couldn't discern if it was because she was making a little too much effort, or stalling.

Quit trying so hard. This isn't a first date. These butterflies are just silly.

Camron hadn't mentioned his marital status, but it was possible he was married and had six kids running around. *Wouldn't that serve me right for taking so long to get ready?*

She walked to the barn to check out the golf cart. It took two hands for her to pull the tall sliding doors open. The barn smelled of hay, but the days when the stalls were filled with horses had passed. It was oddly quiet in the old building.

Rather than tightly cross-stacked squares of hay, huge round bales lined one entire side of the barn. Wrapped in white plastic, in stacks three high, they looked like giant snowmen just waiting for a face and scarf.

It was awkwardly empty without the stacks of feed, seed, and fertilizer on pallets depending upon the season, and Grandpa Johnny's big John Deere tractor was nowhere to be found either. On a positive note, also missing was the pungent smell of diesel fuel.

The light caught something red in her peripheral. There it was. A shiny, candy-apple red golf cart. But this wasn't the standard golf course ride. This thing was more like a dune buggy with big knobby tires.

The key dangled from the ignition.

She slid behind the steering wheel and examined the controls. It didn't look too difficult. A brake and gas pedal. No gears. *What could go wrong?*

Eliana gave the key a twist, and the cart fired up with a throaty gurgle. She took her foot off the brake and pressed the gas pedal. The vehicle bolted forward.

With a squeal, she stomped on the brake and lurched to a stop.

She tried again, this time a little easier, and made it through the doors. The steering was tight, and she was glad no one could see her, because it must look like she'd never driven in her life.

Her path was as crooked as a bee pollinating a field of flowers.

By the time she got by the first paddock, she about had the hang of it and kept a steady speed.

Picturing Grandpa Johnny puttering around on a John Deere tractor was easy, but imagining him zipping around on this radical ride was impossible.

She got to the old bridge, and thoughts of Penny and the day the two of them buried the time capsule came flooding back. It had been brutally hot that summer. So hot they'd gotten dizzy trying to dig the hole.

Eliana slowed to a stop then walked down to the creek's edge. It seemed steeper now, and she turned sideways to keep from losing her balance. She remembered how they'd giggled with excitement as they searched for the right spot.

Is it possible the time capsule could still be intact?

She walked along the bank, trying to remember where they'd buried the thing. It had taken them days, scooping dirt out by the spoonful to make the hole big enough for the army-green ammo box her dad had given them for the task. Made from metal, it had been heavy when it was empty. Once it was filled, it was too heavy for them to carry the long distance. They'd finally had to trust Grandpa Johnny with the location and ask for his help to get it there.

We had some good times down here, Penny. Catching tadpoles. The little turtle that we named Pokey. Sitting in the cold creek water in the summer to cool off. Sorry I didn't get to catch up with you as an adult.

"Who knew all those memories would still be this precious years later?" She pressed her hands together. "I'm sorry we didn't get together."

CHAPTER ELEVEN

Eliana brushed a tear from her cheek as she glanced to where the golf cart sat puttering in the grass. She needed to get a move on if she wasn't going to be late.

Taking a big breath to gather her emotions, she walked back to the cart, pulled down the sun visor, and tapped away the smudged mascara under her eyes. Pressing her foot on the accelerator, she soared up the path with the wind drying her tear-stained cheeks. She kept up her speed until she got to the top of the ridge.

A house with the trendy new-farmhouse look sat where open pastures once lay all the way to Camron's grandparents' house. The shiny black metal roof and black-trim windows accented the white vertical board-and-batten siding. A barn quilt hung to the left of the front door in shades of blue and gray.

Camron waved from the porch.

Even from this far away, she could picture the dimple in his right cheek. That smile was hard to forget.

She gunned it then parked in front of his house. "This place is beautiful!" She climbed out of the golf cart, a little in awe. "Now I can see that it *is* pretty convenient for you to stop and water flowers. You're so close. I just assumed you were living in your grandparents' old place."

"I changed the old homestead into a packaging facility."

"You've expanded."

"I have. Johnny was a big help. It made sense to build the house closer to him. I can't go anywhere in any direction without passing his house. When I traveled, he'd keep an eye on things here."

"Oh! Wait right here." She dashed back to the golf cart and got the gift she'd picked up for him. With the small blue gift bag in hand, she jogged over to where he stood.

"What is that?"

"A little host gift. Since you're cooking for me."

He lit up. "You didn't have to do that." He reached into the bag and pulled out the dish towel, laughing as he read it. "This is great." He wrapped his arms around her and hugged her. "Are you really going to wash dishes?"

"Of course! I always pull my weight."

"I don't doubt that you would. What do you think of that golf cart? Fun, right?"

"This golf cart is awesome," Eliana exclaimed. "It was a little tricky at first, but I love it. I bet you had something to do with this. I can't imagine Grandpa Johnny picking something like this out."

"You'd be right about that. When he was unable to get up on the tractor anymore, he was really depressed. He insisted I accept the John Deere as a gift. I didn't like the idea but said I'd go along with it if I did his bushhogging for him. My tractor was older and persnickety, so I accepted the gift, but when I sold my old tractor, I bought him the golf cart. I gave it to him on his birthday last year."

"That was not only generous but thoughtful."

"I could never repay him for all he did for me. Best I can do is try to pay it forward, I guess."

The way his mouth set showed the depth of his grief. "We had a genuine friendship," he continued. "Built on our mutual love for agriculture and the craftsmanship it takes to care for things on a farm, something Johnny was an expert at."

"I never realized you two were so close." Camron was a lot like Grandpa Johnny. Tears glistened in his eyes, but he didn't move to wipe them away. "You two had an unusual friendship."

"It worked," he said. "Your grandfather was a good man, and I treasured our relationship."

"What can I do to help with dinner?"

"Not a thing. It's pretty much ready now." He invited her into the kitchen.

It was as beautiful as those featured in country-lifestyle magazines. The well-appointed kitchen had all the newest appliances and a gas range a chef would covet. Decorated in red-and-black buffalo plaid with red accents, the room was striking. "Who did your decorating?"

"Do you like it?" he asked.

"Yeah, I do."

"Was that your way of asking if I'm married?"

She laughed. "It is. You got me."

"Married to my work," he said.

"Me too." *And why does that make me happy?*

"Being single isn't as bad as people think."

"Right? I agree." She leaned her forearms on the island between them. "I don't know why everyone thinks you have to be married to be happy."

"Isn't that crazy? An honest day's work is rewarding. I don't need someone else to validate my dreams."

"Happiness doesn't depend on someone else," Eliana said. Although she hadn't done that great of a job at the happy part.

"Only God. Prioritize your faith, family, and friends, and the rest will fall into place when it's supposed to." Camron took the foil off a big hunk of meat. "But honestly, I'm ready for marriage. The right woman just hasn't come along."

She inhaled the smoky smell, her mouth beginning to water. "Barbecue pork?"

"Yep," he said. "I'm known for my recipe around here. I made coleslaw and baked beans too." He sliced the meat and then put spoons in the side dishes. "Help yourself. Don't be shy."

She piled on the food. She hadn't had good barbecue in years.

"I'm glad to see you're not one of those girls who barely eats."

"Well, don't be too impressed. I eat yogurt for breakfast every morning and I walk every day to keep my weight in check."

"Sounds like a healthy lifestyle to me." He sat in the ladder-back chair across from her.

"Well, you know how to treat a girl. Get a load of this dinner."

"I'm trying to impress you."

"It's working."

Camron said grace, and then Eliana looked over at her old friend, happy to be with him again. It was so easy, almost as if she'd never left. "Hey, what happened to Penny? I met her daughter over at the lawyer's office. She said Penny died eight years ago."

"Yeah. It was unexpected. She had a heart attack. No one could believe it. She was in great shape. Rode horses and worked in the yard. She was a stay-at-home mom. You met Christina?"

"Yes. Very sweet girl."

"She's smart. A real go-getter like her mom was. Your grandfather helped her make connections with the right people to help get her landscape company going. She's gonna do good things for this town. She takes truckloads of plants down to Richmond and Norfolk every month, and Johnny financed her buying the old Christmas tree farm. Remember the one over on the hill behind the high school?"

"I do. We used to cut our Christmas trees there."

"We did too. They closed their doors a while back. It's going to take time before it pays off, but Johnny and Christina put together a great long-term plan. Her future looks very bright."

"Penny was like that too. Always thinking about the future, I mean. Did she tell you that when we were kids she and I buried a time capsule down under the bridge?"

"How did I not know that?"

"We pinky-promised we'd open it together when I reached the ripe old age of forty."

They both laughed. "That's not as old as it used to be, is it?" Camron asked.

"It's sad she didn't make it to forty. It seemed like such a long ways away at the time."

He took another forkful of food. "You know, we should go dig it up."

"What?"

"The time capsule. I mean, unless you buried it in a cardboard shoebox, it should still be in good shape."

"Dad gave us an ammo box. After days of working on digging that big hole, I remember we said we should've split the stuff up into several little boxes because it would've been a lot easier to bury."

"Then you probably didn't bury it very deep. That's good news for us." A crooked smile spread, and with a lift of his right brow, he said, "Let's look for it."

"Unless Penny dug it up, which is doubtful, it could still be there," said Eliana. "What do we have to lose?"

Camron grinned. "Not a thing."

"I don't remember what all we put in that box. We picked out some things together, but then we each put something secret in before we had Grandpa Johnny help us seal it up."

"It should be a hoot. Now eat, before it gets cold."

"This is so good. I'm glad you invited me for dinner," she said. "Where'd you learn to cook like this?"

"I'm a bachelor in a town with no takeout. I had no choice."

"Good point."

"Plus, I'm a member of the volunteer fire department, and we take turns cooking. I learned from the best. I kind of stink at cooking for just two though. So plan on taking leftovers home with you."

"Fine by me. If I'm lucky, I'll eke by without cooking at all."

Eliana put her fork down. "I never asked, because it was always so mysterious and Grandpa Johnny was super sensitive about it, but do you know what the big deal is about that cuff link on the mantel?"

Camron nodded. "He told me it was a reminder to himself that things aren't always as they seem and problems have a way of working themselves out."

"That's a lot of philosophical advice gleaned from one lonely cuff link that was considered worthless."

"You're right, but we all have reminders in our lives that keep us focused on the right stuff. I have my grandfather's farm and so many lessons from Johnny."

Loneliness fell over her. She wished she had some little anything to anchor her.

∽ Chapter Twelve ∾

Camron noticed the change in Eliana's demeanor. The glimmer of amusement that had been there just a moment ago flickered out like a flame in a breeze.

"Maybe we're all as useless as a single cuff link in one way or another," Camron said. "As much as I like being single, sometimes I wish I had a matching cuff link, but that's not as easy as it sounds."

She rolled her eyes. "Don't I know it?"

"But it should be." Camron took in a slow breath. "All it takes is being honest about who you are and what you want, right?"

"I'm not sure many people know the answers to those questions."

"Maybe that's the problem. Do you know what you want?" It seemed the question caught her off guard, because she sat there quiet for a long time. He refused to be the one to break the silence.

Finally, she said, "I honestly haven't really thought about it. Maybe I'm afraid of what I'll figure out."

"Oh? Well, at least that's an honest response. When was the last time you did think about it?"

When she laughed, it was like an old song that he hadn't heard in forever. Familiar. Kind of magical. "I'm not sure I can even remember." She stood. "Maybe that's my cue to head on back to the house."

"Wait just one second. I'll walk you out." Camron went into the kitchen and returned with a couple of plastic containers. "Sorry about all the questions. I didn't mean to make you uncomfortable."

"No. It's fine. It's a fair question. One I should probably give some thought to and, as luck would have it, I have some free time. I'll get back to you on it."

"Good. This was going to be served with a sparkler, but you can enjoy it at home just the same." He handed her the smaller of the two containers.

"What is it?"

"You can't guess?"

She lifted the edge, and the smell of buttercream teased her nose immediately. "You're something else. Thank you. This is the perfect ending to a really sweet night."

"You're welcome. I enjoyed it too." He grabbed a jacket off the coatrack by the door as they walked out. "Here. You can borrow this. The air gets damp this time of year."

She slipped her arms into the sleeves. "Thanks." His jacket swallowed her up, hanging well below her hips. She looked so cute he wished she hadn't called it a night. With a slight tilt of her chin, she asked, "So do you want to help me find that time capsule while I'm in town?"

"Definitely. Can I pick you up for the service tomorrow?"

"That would be great. Thank you."

He handed her the container of barbecue, and she walked toward the golf cart, twisting around once to wave before climbing behind the wheel and speeding off into the night.

He stood on the porch until she was out of sight before he turned and went inside.

All the things about Eliana Turner that had intrigued him as a kid still piqued his interest tonight.

She might be my matching cuff link.

What in the world had made him think that?

It wasn't easy finding the perfect farmer's wife. It took a special woman to put up with the constant shuffling of plans due to weather or calving season or retail holiday chaos. Money wasn't consistent. It ebbed and flowed with the market and seasons.

Diversifying his company had made his business strong. Thankfully circumstances had never negatively impacted all three areas—agriculture, wholesale, and retail markets—at the same time. But his life was busy.

What was all the success good for if not to share it with someone? And could he even call himself successful if he'd put himself in a position where he didn't have time to fulfill the part of his dream that included a wife and kids?

For the last seven years he'd been laser-focused on building a stable business. Now here he was with everyone his age he knew already married with children, and he hadn't even come close to finding the right woman.

His thoughts mocked him as a picture of Eliana danced in his mind.

Maybe I always knew who my perfect partner was.

Was there some tiny part of him that had nurtured his friendship with Johnny Turner with Johnny's granddaughter in mind?

No, they were true friends.

Johnny Turner had given him good advice and lessons he couldn't learn from a book. Hands-on experience from an old farmer was simple and easy to take because it wasn't fettered with complications that shouldn't be a part of the equation to begin with. Like modern chemicals that had quick results but long-term negative effects. He'd followed in Johnny's path, leveraging compost and things like chicken manure to buoy his crop production without extra expense. Sure, it was more work. Sure, it even stank to high heaven for a day or two, but nobody could deny he had the best pumpkins around. Plus, he made a better profit because the chicken farmers paid him to remove the litter and he didn't have the expense of buying fertilizer. A win-win.

If I win Eliana's heart, I won't end up like that cuff link.

He took a shower and changed into pajama bottoms. From his window he saw the glow from the upstairs bedroom at Johnny's house. He wondered if Eliana was thinking of him too.

She was probably focused on her memories of the time capsule.

He had a few days to figure out if this was remnants from a schoolboy crush that he should've let go of long ago, or if that spark was a sign of something meant to be.

He walked over to the cherrywood box on his dresser. Johnny had made it for him as a Christmas gift a few years ago. He opened it and shuffled a few loose odds and ends around. Underneath the first hundred-dollar bill he ever got was the little ring that he'd bought that summer for the girl of his dreams. He'd never had the chance to give it to her though. He picked up the small silver-toned circle with a single red stone in the center of the *O* in the word *love*.

"This probably wouldn't impress you much now." He set it back in the box, wondering how he would propose to his one true love when the time came.

❧ Chapter Thirteen ❧

The next morning, Eliana put on her black dress. She didn't even bother with makeup. It wouldn't be there long anyway. She was already crying, and she dreaded the funeral.

She found a handkerchief in Johnny's top drawer to take with her. She let her hand glide along the banister on the way down, imagining all of the Turners over the years who'd walked those stairs.

Camron drove up in a Mercedes.

She got up from the porch and walked to the car, where he held the door for her.

"Whose car?"

"Mine."

"Nice."

"Thank you. I can't afford to drive my truck all over. The fuel mileage is the pits. Plus, I kind of always dreamed of having a red sporty car, and you can't beat German engineering."

Camron was living his dreams, checking off important things. She could take a lesson from him. "Good for you. It's very nice."

He lowered himself into the driver's seat and headed for the church. "I figured this was a more respectable ride, given the circumstances."

"This is going to be a hard day," she said.

He slowed to a stop and placed his hand on her arm. "We'll get through it together."

She believed him.

The parking lot was filling fast, and it was still early.

They walked in, taking a quiet moment before the others would be allowed to enter.

Reed met them and shook Camron's hand. "Good morning. I'm glad to see you're here together. Supporting one another in this difficult time." He nodded toward the door. "It's going to be a full house. I can feel the outpouring of the community. One thing's for sure, no one will ever forget Johnny Turner's role in it."

"Thank you," Eliana said quietly. "Everything looks lovely." Flowers filled the front of the church. Cascading sprays, potted plants, and wreaths lined both sides.

The service a half hour later was touching. Pastor Reed read from Grandpa Johnny's Bible, his words as comforting as God's hand.

They sang from the hymnal, and when they were done, Reed said, "It's unsettling to be singing without Johnny's baritone reverberating in our ears. Life will never be the same."

Eliana and Camron sat shoulder to shoulder in the first pew as people shared stories of their precious memories with Grandpa Johnny. Her handkerchief was a damp wad in her hand by the time the service was over and she and Camron had met with friends and received their condolences.

"Everyone loved him so much. What an honor to live a life that touched so many hearts," Eliana said as they walked back to the car.

When he opened the car door for her, she said, "I don't have an ounce of energy left in me."

"Why don't you come stay at my house?" he offered. "I have two extra bedrooms. At least you won't be alone."

The offer was appealing, but she couldn't. There were too many feelings competing for her attention. She just wanted to crawl in bed and be alone.

She walked downstairs in her pajamas unsure if it was still Saturday, or if she'd slept all night long. Her phone showed it was Sunday morning. There were several missed calls, but she didn't even check them. Coffee was about all she could handle at the moment, but when she got to the kitchen doorway, something seemed off. She ignored the feeling and started the coffee.

It brewed in a noisy gurgle, and after a few minutes she filled her cup and carried it with her to go to the porch. In the living room, she suddenly had a strange sensation. She stopped, wondering if it was from sleeping so long, but something drew her toward the mantel.

She walked over and stepped on something sharp. Hopping on one foot, she saw a bright red drop of blood on the hardwood floor.

"Ouch." She dropped to the couch to check her foot. She must have not gotten all the glass up the other day when she dropped the cuff link jar. She squeezed the injury, trying to see if the sliver was visible. One thing she never was good at was blood.

Woozy, she picked up her phone and texted Camron.

I NEED HELP. CUT MY FOOT. CAN YOU COME?

ON THE WAY.

With nothing else to sop up the blood, she dragged the blanket from the back of the couch and pressed it to her foot. *Please hurry.*

Camron burst through the door a moment later, carrying a first-aid kit. "How bad is it?"

"I don't know. I can't stand the sight of blood."

"Relax. You're so stiff you look like you're going to explode."

"I hate blood," she repeated.

"I can see that, but you've got plenty of it still in you. Let me get this cleaned up." He ran to the kitchen and got paper towels.

She leaned back on the couch and took long, deep breaths.

He was able to pull the sliver of glass from her foot, clean the wound, and wrap it in gauze and an elastic wrap. "You can open your eyes."

"Do I need stitches?"

"No. It's not bad at all. You're going to be fine."

"Thank you for rescuing me."

"Hardly a rescue." He laughed. "It'll be tender for a bit though."

She sat up.

"How'd you get glass in your foot?"

"I broke that jar that was over the cuff link on the mantel the other day. Reed was here and helped me clean it up. I guess we didn't do too good a job."

She stared at the mantel. "Hey. Where is the cuff link?"

"It probably fell behind something."

She shook her head. "No, I distinctly remember setting it back on the wooden block."

"Calm down. It has to be here somewhere."

"Maybe I should call the sheriff," she said.

"No. It'll turn up," Camron said. "It's highly unlikely someone would've stolen it."

"That does seem odd." She shrugged. "You're right, it'll turn up. It's been a tough week. Maybe I moved it for some reason. Although I can't think of one."

He glanced at his watch. "I've got to get to church. Do you still want to come with me?"

She hesitated, but then she said, "Yes. I'd love to go to church with you."

"Great. When we get back, we'll go find that time capsule. Let's get your mind cleared. I'll help you search for the cuff link afterward."

"That sounds like a great idea. I could use something happy right now. I'll go get dressed."

It only took a couple of minutes for her to change into a dress and twist her hair into a braid. "Ready."

Camron drove them to the church in his truck, and they slipped into a pew as Reed stepped to the pulpit. "Just in time," Camron whispered.

Eliana grabbed the hymnal and tucked the bulletin between the pages of the first song listed on the hymn board. She was surrounded by people she'd seen at yesterday's service for Grandpa Johnny. Reed's service was uplifting and encouraging, and she felt as welcome today as she had when she'd been a member of this church and attended every Sunday.

Afterwards, many offered not only their condolences, but their help and hopes that she might stay in Burnt Chimney.

One woman said, "I know this is a small town, but we're growing, and there are so many wonderful new things happening. People from Smith Mountain Lake frequent the few shops we have, and we're working on a museum and arts building to get more traffic from people heading to the parkway. By the way, if you have any antique or vintage items from Burnt Chimney's past, Danny Goad will pay you a fair price for them. He's got big plans for that museum."

"I'll keep that in mind, but I don't think I have anything he'd be interested in."

"Oh, I know there were several things he wanted. Your grandfather wasn't ready to part with them, but you might not care."

"I don't know," Eliana said.

"He's been looking for pictures of ancestors, and the Turner family was a big part of the incident that gave this town its name. Danny and your grandfather discussed that."

"I couldn't part with anything at the moment, but I'll keep his name in mind." Eliana wondered if it was possible Danny Goad was responsible for the missing cuff link.

"I'll tell him we spoke and that you'll be reaching out to him."

Eliana politely refrained from commenting again. The woman was downright pushy. If Mr. Goad was anything like her, she saw why her grandfather had refused to give up any of his precious memories.

She turned, searching for Camron. She was ready to leave.

A moment later, he grabbed her hand as he walked by and then took off running.

Her short legs pumped hard to keep up with his longer stride.

They reached the truck, laughing. "Come on," Camron said. "We've got a treasure to find, missy."

"Aye." She did her best pirate accent.

On the way home she asked Camron if he knew anything about Danny Goad and the museum project.

Camron rolled his eyes. "He means well, but Burnt Chimney's origin story isn't the most pleasant one for the Turner family. Your grandfather wasn't excited about it, especially because this guy wanted to use it to attract tourists, not for the historical value."

"What do you think?"

"I think it all happened a long time ago and tourists would probably enjoy learning about the history, but I understand Johnny's sensitivity about it."

"Is it possible this Goad guy stole the cuff link?"

Camron shook his head. "No. He's a good man. I've done business with him. I can't see it."

"Well then, what happened to it? I just can't understand how it would go completely missing all by itself."

"Be patient. It'll turn up. I promise we'll find it," he said as he drove up in front of Johnny's house.

"I'll run inside and change," she said.

"And I'll get everything we need for the recovery mission. Meet you back here."

"Ten-four." Anxious to start looking for the time capsule, she ran upstairs and tugged on her khakis, telling herself she could replace the designer pants if she ruined them. Then she found one of Grandpa Johnny's John Deere T-shirts to wear. She hoped excavating the time capsule would be easier than burying it.

When she got downstairs, Camron had already pulled the golf cart around. In the back was a shovel, a pickax, a rake, and a couple of five-gallon buckets.

"It's hard to say if years of runoff down to the creek would've packed more mud on top of your hiding spot or washed it away, but we'll be prepared either way," he said.

"I like the way you think," Eliana said. "This is going to be like getting a go-back card to our childhood."

"I can't think of a better place for us to pick up where we left off." Camron winked and tooted the horn on the golf cart. "Come on. Let's do this."

"I wouldn't miss it for the world." She hopped into the seat next to him, wondering if she'd ever in her whole life felt more happy than at this moment.

CHAPTER FOURTEEN

Camron was captivated by Eliana, and not only with her beauty, but with the energy and confidence that the grown-up version now displayed so elegantly. He couldn't imagine a better place to be.

"Let's go!" she yelled.

"Wait, we're missing one important tool."

She scanned the contents of the cart. "What are we missing?"

"The secret weapon." He took off in a jog to his truck and dropped the tailgate. "This should guarantee us success."

Her brows knit. "What is that?"

"A metal detector. After we talked about the time capsule the other night, I dug this out of my shed."

"I don't know why on earth you'd have one of those, but it's genius."

"If you own as many acres as I do, you're bound to need it occasionally." He set the metal detector in the back of the cart. "Had to look for my watch once, tools all the time. I'm terrible about laying them down and losing track of them, and on occasion I find things that aren't even mine."

"We're all set. Hey, wait a minute. Can we use that to find the cuff link?"

Camron snapped his fingers. "Well, yes. It'll pick up gold."

"Come on. Bring it now."

He retrieved the metal detector, and after twenty minutes of sweeping through the living room and even checking the floor vents—although Camron was quite certain the cuff link wouldn't have fit through the slots—they had to admit it wasn't there.

Eliana walked out of the house and got in the golf cart.

"Don't be disappointed," Camron said.

"I can't help it. I shouldn't have messed with it."

He laughed. "Do you think Johnny is hiding it to punish you?"

"He might be," she said with a hint of laughter in her voice. "He was always very serious about me not touching it."

"I'm kidding. Good to see you smile though." Camron started the golf cart and headed up the path, skidding to a stop when they got to the bridge.

They both bailed out. Eliana's chime-like giggle filled the air. "I can't believe how excited I am. I mean, it's just old worthless junk."

"It's memories. You can't put a price on that."

"True. I hope there are some good ones in there. I have to warn you, my childhood wasn't as storybook as yours."

"Eliana, all families have secrets and challenges."

"I just… Well, I don't know what I put in that time capsule, but I'd rather you not be surprised by anything I might have written."

"I'd never judge you. I kind of know, from Johnny. I'm sorry for all you had to endure."

"No, I'm the one who's sorry. I shouldn't have brought it up." She shifted back to her smiling self. "Come on. How do we use that metal detector?"

"It's a little heavy. Need me to do it?"

"I can do it. Show me how."

Camron walked her through the steps then helped her start scanning near the bridge where they'd buried the time capsule all those years ago. After a few minutes he took off his watch and laid it on the grass. "Come scan this so you can hear what it sounds like when you find something."

"Oh goodness! That's easy. I've got it."

He slipped his watch back onto his wrist then went to the golf cart and pulled a long slim metal rod from the rear seat. He used it to poke holes in the ground along the bank, hoping to strike something hard. "How far from the water line were y'all?"

"I have no idea. I just remember us believing that the bridge was going to protect it in some way." She walked slowly, swinging the apparatus from side to side, listening for a signal.

For a good thirty minutes, they both hunted in silence. The afternoon sun was warm, and in the distance, he could see his cows moving across the pasture toward the shade like they were known to do about this time of day.

Suddenly, Eliana called, "I think I found something!"

Camron grabbed the shovel and ran over to help her. He turned over a scoop of dirt. "See if it's in the dirt I just turned or if it's still in the ground."

She positioned the metal detector over both spots. "To the right of where you dug."

He moved the shovel to the right and turned over another shovelful.

She tested it. "It's still there, but now to the left."

He shrugged. "Well, your time capsule would have to be pretty little to fit in this small space."

"Oh yeah." Her lips pursed. "This isn't going to be easy."

"But we've got something." He squatted and started sifting through the dirt. She knelt beside him and helped.

He saw something metal and tugged on it.

"What is that?"

"I believe this is a cowbell." He shook it. "Without a clacker."

"Still fun. Well, at least we found something."

They got back to work, and it wasn't long before he noticed she was beginning to struggle with keeping the metal detector at a steady height.

"Can I switch jobs with you for a bit?"

"Yes, please. Thank you."

He took over and worked his way to the bottom of the bridge, where finally he got a strong signal. "Eliana, I think we've got it. Bring that rod with you."

She raced over and handed it to him. "How do you know?"

"See how the signal is strong here...and over here? It's a big object."

"Bigger than a cowbell. That's got to be it!"

Camron dug the heel of his shoe in the dirt to mark where the signal was strongest and then began digging. He turned up three shovelfuls before he finally hit something hard.

Eliana grabbed his arm. "That's it. Right?"

"I think so. See if you can uncover it to the edges."

She knelt and plunged her hands into the loose dirt, sweeping handfuls to the side. "It's the box. I'd know that green anywhere. Even dirty!" She looked up, her hair falling across her right eye. "Good enough?"

"Yes. I can see it now."

She scooched back from the hole and let him dig out the area around the container.

Twenty years of rain and erosion must have piled more dirt over it, because it was in deep.

All in all, it took another half hour for Camron to free the old ammo box from the ground. On the side of it was puff-painted TIME CAPSULE PENNY AND ELIANA.

"Quite the little artist, weren't you?" Camron said.

"I'd forgotten we did that. I think it was Penny's idea. She always had all the cool craft stuff at her house."

"It's cute." And so was Eliana, filthy right up to her elbows, a smudge of dirt next to her nose, and big round stains on her knees from kneeling in the mud.

She must have noticed him looking her over, because she swiped at her pants and said, "We're a mess!"

"Definitely a dirty job, but we did it." He raised his hand, and she high-fived him.

"I think I'd like to be a treasure hunter," she said. "This is exciting."

"It is, but I'm hungry, and I don't want to be tempted to eat anything that's been in that box for two decades."

"Me too. Come on. We can throw some hot dogs on the grill."

"You got a deal." He lifted the time capsule and carried it over to the golf cart. "I can't wait to see what y'all packed into this thing. It feels like it's full of rocks."

"I remember Grandpa Johnny commenting about how heavy it was the day he helped us bury it."

They drove to Johnny's house. After parking in the driveway, he said, "I can get the hot dogs on the grill if you want to go and get cleaned up."

"I'm a mess. Thanks. I'll be quick."

"Sure. I've got this. Take your time." While she went upstairs, he took everything they'd need out on to the deck and lit the gas grill. He rolled hot dogs across the grates, careful to keep them from burning, although he didn't mind them that way.

When she walked outside, the way her damp hair waved in tendrils across her shoulders took his attention for a moment too long, and he let the fire flame up.

"How did you know I like mine a little charred?"

He scooched them off the hottest part of the flame and pretended it was intentional. "Anything to please."

She took the twist-tie off the bag of hot dog buns. "How many for you?"

"Two."

She put the buns on paper plates and opened a bag of chips.

"They're ready." He turned off the grill and used the tongs to put the hot dogs on their plates.

"It's been forever since I've had a good hot dog," she said.

He put potato chips then a hot dog in his bun, drizzled a thin line of mustard along the top, and took a big bite. "I was even hungrier than I realized. I cooked them all, so there's plenty."

She nodded as she chewed. "It's good."

The sun settled on the horizon, casting pink, orange, and golden streaks across the Virginia sky.

"Thank you, Camron. This hits the spot, and isn't it gorgeous? I'm not sure I've seen such a colorful sunset before."

"No two are the same."

"I guess that's the beauty of it," she said. Then, in barely a whisper, she said, "I wish I'd never had to leave. I was really depressed when Mom packed us up. I didn't even know where we were going."

"I missed you. Everyone did. Your dad missed you. He loved you, Eliana. Knowing how your mother bad-mouthed everything about Burnt Chimney, no telling what she said. When you left, a lot of us lost something. Your dad was a wreck. He moved in with Johnny. Everyone was worried about him."

"I wish I'd known that. I'm not happy that he was sad about it, but I believed for so long that he didn't care. Or didn't care enough."

"That's simply not true."

Her lips quivered, but she smiled.

"Are you about ready to reveal the contents of that time capsule?" Camron asked.

She rubbed her hands together. "Ready as I'll ever be."

Camron went and got the time capsule and set it on the picnic table with a thud. "It's all you, my friend."

Eliana slipped her fingers under the latch on the side of the box and tried to lift it, but it didn't budge even a smidgen. "I might need some help."

"Those old army ammo boxes have a pretty good vacuum seal on them. We'll do it together. Ready?"

He placed his hands on top of hers and they pulled, the lid finally giving up its grip and opening.

She let out a squeal of delight. "Yes!"

Her hands were warm beneath his. Their eyes locked for a moment.

She hitched a breath that made his heart staccato.

Camron grinned. "Let's see what's inside."

She removed a white envelope from the very top. In straight block letters, ELIANA & PENNY was written in blue ink.

She turned the envelope over in her hand. "I don't think this is my handwriting." She lifted the flap up enough to get her finger beneath it, slid out the piece of paper, and shoved it in his direction. "You read it."

Camron unfolded the paper and read, "'Girls, you were so excited to bury this time capsule. You wouldn't even tell me what was in it. I hope I'm around when you open it, but if I'm not, I want you both to know that your friendship and the smiles on your faces as you worked tirelessly to put this together have brought me so much joy. I know you both will be beautiful, successful, and capable women. I hope all your dreams come true. Love, Grandpa Johnny.'"

A tear slipped down Eliana's cheek. "That's so sweet."

"There are two one-hundred-dollar bills." He twisted them between his fingers. "They would go a lot further back then."

"True enough." She lifted the next thing in the box. A folded-up copy of the local newspaper.

They opened the circular flyer, laughing at the ridiculously low prices just twenty years ago.

"This will be fun to read through as an adult."

"I doubt we were even aware of what was going on out in the real world back then," Camron said.

Camron and Eliana took turns pulling things out of the box. A CD with her and Penny's favorite Christian songs, a drawing of the characters in *Finding Nemo*, postage stamps, their report cards, and a picture of the two of them in a bejeweled popsicle-stick picture frame that Penny had made in vacation Bible school that summer.

Camron snagged her report card from her. "I knew it. You got all As."

"Always did."

"I'm not surprised."

"Look. I do remember this." She revealed a very tarnished silver heart-shaped jewelry box that held some colored rubber bands she'd used on her braces and a gold cross on a thin chain.

"I remember you wearing that cross to church."

"My dad bought it for me when I was little. The chain was too short for me to wear it anymore by the time I put it in here."

"That's an easy fix. What's that?" He pointed to an envelope.

"It looks like one of our notes to ourselves. We each wrote one." She peered closer at the envelope. "This is Penny's." She placed that one in her lap. "I have to get this to Penny's daughter. We should let her be the one to open it, don't you think?"

"She'll appreciate that," Camron agreed.

A red shop rag, like the ones Grandpa Johnny always had tucked in his back pocket, was tied with a slip of light blue ribbon.

"You used to wear that ribbon in your hair," he said.

"I did. How do you remember that?"

He didn't want to make it awkward, but he had to tell her. "Eliana, every little detail about you is etched in my memory. You were the first girl I ever fell in love with, even though we were so young, and even now you make me act like a teenager."

She rolled her eyes. "Right," she said with a laugh.

"Eliana. I'm serious." His heart pounded harder.

"Oh? Really?"

"Yes. You don't feel the least little anything between us?"

She caught her breath. "I haven't thought about it like that. It's been more than twenty years since we've seen each other. I'm busy. I don't have time for dating, or anything, in my life. I—"

"Johnny worried about that. He talked about it all the time. Surely you want to find that special someone someday, don't you?"

She lowered her eyes. "You know, my parents made a mess of things. I think it's just not in my DNA."

"That's ridiculous. Everyone needs and deserves love."

"I wouldn't begin to know how to start."

"Like this. Sharing. Laughing. That's all there is to getting to know someone."

"But if you let that happen, you can get hurt too." She pressed her lips together. "You have no idea how much it hurt when Mom took me away."

"You were gone from the fighting and arguing. That had to be better. Wasn't it?"

"No, because even though that was over, she constantly complained about everything. Dad and my grandparents were the only ones who ever showed me love. There were never hugs or goodnight kisses once we left. Not even kind words unless it was in response to something about her."

He placed his hand on her arm. "I'm sorry you had to live through that. It will never be like that again for you if I have anything to say about it. Believe that."

Her happiness was what mattered most. He liked being with her, and he wasn't ready for it to end. He had to convince her she belonged here, even if it was only for friendship.

CHAPTER FIFTEEN

Eliana's heart raced, the weight of Camron's statement pressing on her. When she'd told Mom she missed Camron when they got to California, Mom called it puppy love and made her feel stupid for thinking he could have been interested in her.

I wasn't stupid. It was real.

She looked at him again through the lens of that little girl, remembering how much she loved being at her grandparents' house, playing with her best friends.

A slight blush reddened his cheeks. "Sounds kind of silly all these years later, but I wouldn't have expected my feelings to still be so strong for you."

"Maybe it's just us missing Grandpa Johnny. You two were best friends. I'm his granddaughter. We have that connection."

He shook his head insistently. "No. That's not it."

She shrugged. "I don't know what to say."

"Say you'll let me be here for you through all of this. Stay for a while, and let's see where it goes."

"And if it goes nowhere?"

"At the very least, we'll always share this bond with Johnny. And we'll always be friends."

But the conversation left her a bit dizzy. "How about we pick up the rest of this excavation tomorrow? I'm suddenly tired."

He looked disappointed. "Sure. Yeah. Tomorrow. How about we meet here for breakfast? I'll bring the eggs."

"That sounds nice."

"Thanks for including me in the dig. What do you think about inviting Christina over tomorrow to see it? I'll put some burgers on the grill for lunch."

"That's a great idea." Although she'd just committed to breakfast and lunch with a man who pretty much confessed his childhood crush on her. It seemed like this was moving a bit too fast, but then, if Grandpa Johnny were here, wouldn't he want her to be friends with his best friend?

"I'll give her a call. She should be planning to come cut flowers tomorrow anyway. She usually does that every other Monday."

"She harvests flowers here? For her business?"

"Johnny had an elaborate plan for the flower field. We spent two years getting it right. He was very particular about it."

Eliana was shocked that her grandfather had never mentioned it, especially since the two of them had spent so much time planning her imaginary cut flower business together. "I've got to see that."

"I'll take you down tomorrow. I'll contact Christina and see what her plans are." Camron got up. "You stay put. I'll show myself out."

The next morning, Eliana woke up and walked outside. It was so peaceful listening to the birds and doing nothing more than watching the dew dry. All she had on her agenda was to wait for Camron, who'd promised her a fresh egg breakfast.

She sat there for a good little while, watching the sun rise and crisscross the mountains and the shadows on the grass. It was still early, and if she had to guess, Camron had a lot of morning chores running a dairy farm.

She slipped on her shoes and headed out to where the land sloped behind the barn, where she'd once dreamed of running a cut flower farm.

When she got to the ridge, the old burnt chimney rose in the distance, the one this town was named after. But in this pasture, or what used to be one, there were rows and rows of beautiful blooms. Bold purple, soft pink, a light lavender, and an array of reds and pinks framed in white. A blanket of solid yellow flowers filled at least an acre rectangle, and it looked so soft that she was tempted to run down the hill and roll in them.

It was as beautiful as the images she'd dreamed of as a girl. Could it be possible the long rows of white were Fantasia freesias like in the plans she and Grandpa Johnny had made?

Was it her imagination, or could she smell them from here?

She'd fallen in love with the fragrance of the beautiful white blossoms known for lasting weeks. Granny Mae had a round bed of them in the front yard. When Eliana would play on the tree swing, the higher she went, the more she smelled them. She loved picking them and bringing them inside for Granny Mae, who always lavished her with praise for being so thoughtful. Together, they'd arrange them in a vase, and then Granny Mae would wrap an arm around Eliana's shoulders and squeeze her in the sweetest way.

She missed that feeling.

Eliana started down the hill, the steep angle pushing her almost into a jog.

When she got to the bottom, she ran straight up the middle row to the center of the flower field then stopped and stood there in awe of the beauty.

Emotion coursed through her, almost too much to contain. Her little-girl dream was alive and thriving right here in Burnt Chimney without her. *And I didn't even know it.*

Bees bounced in and out of the pretty petals. She spotted the beehives Camron had mentioned against the tree line. Some of them were stacked like little condos five stories high.

The building they'd used for Granny Mae's hackney ponies was now a potting shed, just like she'd mapped out. She remembered how patient Grandpa Johnny had been, helping her create the budget. Every detail, down to the siding, work benches, and irrigation had been planned for.

Eliana's phone rang. "Hey, Camron. I'm in the flower field. I'll be right up." She tucked her phone in her back pocket and headed up the hill, picking a few more flowers along the way.

Camron stood on the porch, smiling.

"Those for me?" he asked, nodding toward the bouquet in her hand.

"Could be. Want to help me get them in some water?"

"Sure." He followed her inside, carrying a carton of eggs. "I called Christina and invited her to come earlier than usual and join us for breakfast. She should be here any minute."

"Perfect timing. I'm starving." She started fussing with the flowers, trimming the stems and tucking each one into the vase. "Coffee should still be hot."

He helped himself to a cup then switched on the gas stove. He had cheese omelets plated before she finished the bouquet.

"Knock, knock," Christina called from the screen door.

"Come on in," Eliana called out.

Christina came in carrying a covered dish. "Hope y'all like cinnamon rolls. It's about the only breakfast food I know how to cook."

She set them on the table, and Camron carried the omelets over.

"Grab a cup of coffee, Christina. Let's eat while it's hot," Eliana said.

"Thanks," Christina said. "How are you this morning, Eliana?"

"I'm doing okay. I got up early, so I walked down to the flower field."

"Isn't it amazing?" Christina said. "I've got to cut flowers this afternoon. You can help if you want. Your grandfather modeled that field after a business plan he helped you with when you were just a kid."

It meant so much to her to know he'd been thinking of her when he planted it.

"I guess those checks will go directly to you now," Christina said, lifting a cinnamon roll out of the pan and onto her plate.

"What checks?"

Camron and Christina looked at each other.

"What am I missing?" Eliana waited for an explanation.

Christina licked icing from her finger before saying, "After I graduated from college and started my greenhouse, your grandfather was helping me get my business plan in place. That's when he told me about your dream of having a cut flower farm. He never told you this?"

"No. Not a word."

"Well, I assumed you knew about it. He decided to put your amazing plan into action and allowed me to buy the cut flowers from here. I distribute them all over the state. I have a greenhouse for houseplants and acreage with shrubs and trees, and he helped me get the old Christmas tree farm back on its feet. It's still not making a profit, but I did sell a truckload of small trees last year for a premium."

"This is amazing. How did you do all that?"

"He had Camron till and prep the soil, and the three of us worked together."

"We hired 4-H'ers to come help us plant all those flower seeds and bulbs," Camron said. "We got help, and they got fancy gardening badges."

"It was a long process," Christina said. "Mostly because he was fastidious about it. It had to be just like you planned."

"When did that all happen? It's a wonderful stand of flowers. It's well established."

"Five years ago?" Camron said. "Johnny put a lot of time and thought into the project. Bottom line is that Christina comes and cuts flowers and sells them to buyers all over North Carolina and Virginia, and Johnny gets a cut."

"Cute pun. He gets a cut from the cut flowers. I see what you did there, Camron," Christina teased. "I hope I'm not overstepping, Eliana, but I think your grandfather always hoped you'd come back and run the flower farm."

"But he never told me about it. That doesn't make sense."

"Maybe he just ran out of time." Camron pushed his empty plate away. "Time is our most precious commodity. None of us knows how much of it we'll have."

It was a truth she hadn't done a good job of remembering. *God, I'm listening. I hear the messages.* And she could feel them too.

Chapter Sixteen

After breakfast, Eliana, Christina, and Camron unpacked the rest of the time capsule.

Christina read the letter that her mother had written to her future self, crying quiet tears with a smile playing on her lips as she did so. "I feel so close to her right now. She did all the things she'd hoped to do. Married a wonderful man, had a daughter, taught me to love nature the way she did, and to give back to this community. It wasn't fancy, but it was exactly what she dreamed of." She folded the letter and tucked it back in the envelope. "I can't thank you enough for sharing this with me."

Christina pressed the envelope to her heart. "Mom was such a sweet little girl," she continued. "It's hard to think of her as being young, but she had the same wit and wisdom then as she did the day she died. I'm so thankful that you dug this up. Can I keep this?"

"Of course," Eliana said. "It's yours. You remind me so much of her. I wish I'd known you before. All the times I snuck home to see Grandpa Johnny, I didn't even try to see Penny. I wish I had. I guess I had tunnel vision."

Eliana barely remembered her childhood dreams. She hadn't thought about them at all until this week. Her life was okay. She had a great job. It paid well, and she had money saved and a corporate match on her retirement and 401(k) that should have her set for retirement when she finally got there.

"Did you write one too?" Christina asked.

"I did, but I haven't read it yet."

"As soon as we're done eating, we need to go look through the rest of the capsule." Christina looked excited.

Camron was the first to finish, and he cleared his plate and cleaned up the pans he'd cooked in. Eliana picked up her plate and Christina's and put them in the sink.

"Everything is in here," Eliana said, walking toward the dining room. Camron and Christina followed.

"I'm so thankful Mom lived her perfect life," Christina said. "She inspired me to try new things. I knew exactly what my gifts were early on, and she encouraged me to figure out how to put the things I naturally loved to good use. I work hard, but it's so rewarding I don't mind."

How was it that this young woman was so comfortable in her skin and could run her own business in such a grown-up and successful way? *When am I going to figure all that out?*

Observing Camron and Christina, she could see Grandpa Johnny's giving ways mirrored in them.

She wanted to be more like that. Her life seemed so lonely compared to theirs. Something that had never bothered her before.

"The irrigation needs to be turned on. I'm going to do that while y'all go through those things," Camron said.

Eliana walked over and sat at the table. The other items in the box were painted rocks, lists of their favorite candy, and some tiny trinkets that at one time meant something. Beneath a little white pocket-sized Bible was an envelope with the words, *Eliana's Note to Her Future Self.*

Tears tickled her eyes. She opened the envelope, almost afraid to see what she'd written.

To my older self,

Penny and I pinky-promised we'd open this time capsule together when I turn forty. Right now, I'm twelve years old. I love school. I'm good at math, and my teachers are terrific. Penny is my best friend. I really like Camron Carter, but he doesn't know that. He's super cute, but he's really popular, so we're just friends.

Maybe someday I'll meet someone like him and I'll be brave enough to tell him I like him. I want a dog, but Mom says no. Dad wouldn't mind. Mom and Dad fight a lot, so I spend as much time as I can with Granny Mae and Grandpa Johnny. I love spending time with them, and Granny Mae is trying to teach me to bake, but I'm not very good at it. I burned brownies yesterday, but Grandpa Johnny pretended to like them. I thought they were awful. I'd rather be on the farm with him. Being outside is fun, and he buys me all the flower seeds and bulbs I want and teaches me how to plant them. Someday I will have acres of flowers, and people will be so happy to buy them from me. They might drive for hours just for the chance to pick flowers from my garden.

Making other people happy would be the best thing in the world. Especially little girls who are sad. Someday I hope to

*have a little girl. I will be a good mother, and my husband
and I will never fight in front of her.*

*I will always live right here in Burnt Chimney so I can
be close to Grandpa Johnny and Penny and Camron.*

Happy future,

Eliana Turner

ET+CC 4Ever

She stared at the initials and *4Ever.*

Her cheeks warmed. Thank goodness she hadn't read this in
front of Camron.

In the very bottom, as if it had been tucked down the side, was a
bank envelope containing two silver-dollar coins and a letter dated
two years ago.

Dear Eliana,

*You made me promise not to tell anyone about the time
capsule. I didn't, but I did dig it up and sneak this note inside
for you, just in case I'm not there when you finally open it
when you turn forty like you planned.*

*You always asked about the single cuff link on the man-
tel, and why, if one would think it was useless, would I keep it
on display? We didn't talk about it much, because it was a
black eye in our family history.*

*But it was that single cuff link that saved us. It freed my
great-grandfather from being prosecuted for a crime he didn't
commit. For all the mystery around that cuff link, the details
are public record, but nobody talks about it.*

I am the great-grandson of Everett and Nannie Turner. This town was called Burnt Chimney following the fire that took Nannie's store so many years ago. The chimney where you used to play was all that was left. It's an important legacy, and our family has been a good and important part of this community for a long time.

Honey, I know you had a hard start, and you may tie some of those memories to this town, but you are part of this heritage. It's part of who you are, and you belong in this beautiful place.

That gold cuff link belonged to Everett's brother, Edward Turner. It was a gift from his wife. His initials were ET, just like my great-grandfather's, and it was almost enough evidence for Everett to go to jail for burning down Nannie's store. But he'd have never done that. He loved her with all his heart.

You have grown into a beautiful woman. I'm very proud of you. I want you to know that no matter what has happened in our past, it doesn't sully the life God planned for us way before He ever knew us. Don't carry the past around like an anchor. Trust God's love and the love He places in your path.

The time we spent mapping out your dreams for the flower farm were some of the best moments of my life. I loved seeing your heart in that work. When your mother took you away, I clung to those memories. Eliana, I built that farm, and it is exactly as you planned it. I hope you see it someday and that it is exactly as you would have wanted it to be.

I love you. You are a lovely soul. Share your gifts, my dear.

With love,

Grandpa Johnny

"Now I feel even worse about the lost cuff link," she said.

"Who else has been to the house?" Camron asked.

"Reed accidently swept it up and almost threw it away when he helped me clean up the glass."

"No way he could have taken it. He's a pastor and the most honest man I know."

"Plus, he wasn't trying to hide it. It was there in plain sight when he walked by me."

"Who else?"

"I don't know. I slept hard the night after the funeral. I guess anyone could have come in and I wouldn't have heard them." She shook her head. "I feel like I let him down."

She reread the letter then held it close to her heart.

Camron walked over and pulled her into his arms. "I'm sorry, Eliana. I will make sure we get to the bottom of this. Soon."

Chapter Seventeen

On Tuesday morning, Camron called Eliana. "Did you get a text from Nelson Luther?"

"I did. I was just going to get dressed and head to Rocky Mount. How did you know?"

"I got one too. Can I pick you up? We can go together."

"Sure. That would be great," Eliana said. "I can be ready in ten minutes."

In ten minutes on the dot, Camron drove up to the front of Johnny's house. Eliana walked out wearing a flowery dress. Her hair was pulled back, and Camron was certain he'd never laid eyes on a more beautiful woman.

"Good morning," she said as she got in his truck.

"Hey. You look pretty. I like your dress."

She looked surprised. "Thank you." She fussed with her skirt, straightening it across her lap.

Camron tried to keep his attention on the road. It wouldn't take long to get to Nelson's office.

When they walked into the attorney's office together, Christina was already sitting in the reception area.

"Hello again," she said. "So, did you both get texts this morning too?"

"We did. He changed my meeting time," Eliana said.

Nelson Luther stepped out of his office. He was a lanky man who was graying at the temples and wearing black wire-rimmed glasses.

"Good morning. I'm sorry about all the strange charades. Miss Turner, I owe you an apology. I'd never stand up a client. I promise you that I'm a professional, but I was carrying out your grandfather's wishes to the letter. I suppose the three of you have had the chance to meet in my absence."

"We have," said Eliana. "You mean to tell me that Grandpa Johnny arranged for you to have a family emergency?"

"Technically, I suppose it was your family emergency. Not mine."

"I have no idea what's going on here, Nelson," Camron said.

"Please come in and sit down," the lawyer said. "I'll clear all of this up."

The three of them followed him into the office. It was a nice space with one wall lined with floor-to-ceiling bookcases and what looked like a twelve-foot ladder on a rail to get to the books at the very top.

Nelson settled behind a monstrosity of a wooden desk with ornate carvings on the skirt and thick legs. He pushed his glasses up on his nose. "Johnny Turner was a meticulously organized man. His brain worked like a flowchart. He could piece things together quickly and never missed a thing. So you can imagine what I've been dealing with since his death." He lifted a thick folder. "Step-by-step instructions conveying his last wishes."

"No surprise there," Eliana said.

"He was one of my first clients. His last will and testament was my first legal document when I joined the firm. I have a feeling the partners tossed him my way because of his particularly keen eye for detail. They knew if I missed something, he wouldn't." Nelson laughed. "Between us, I think Johnny did most of the work on that first draft. Anyway, we've made adjustments to it over the years, but it wasn't until about a year ago that he came to me with these very specific instructions."

He passed a folder to each of them.

"I've already talked to Reed. He gathered the things your grandfather requested for his funeral. That's already been taken care of, of course." He pulled his glasses off. "I was at the funeral, up in the balcony, at his request. I wouldn't have missed it, and I surely would not want you to think I hadn't paid my respects. I respected Johnny very much, Eliana."

"Thank you." Eliana smiled in Camron's direction.

He wanted to hold her hand, but he hesitated.

"While the three of you were meeting by well-planned accident," Nelson said, smiling, "I was fishing—per Johnny's orders—on some lakefront property off Crestview Road."

"You have lakefront property?" Camron asked.

"No. Johnny does. Did. It's lovely. Prettiest view around. You and Eliana will find out soon enough. There are two small cabins, a covered boat dock, and a pier. He's left the property jointly to you."

Camron and Eliana looked at each other.

"I know," Nelson said. "Neither of you even knew he owned it. That's because he didn't until recently. He's asked that you own it together and that it should never be sold but rather paid forward to someone in your future who will do the same. He wants both of you to commit to spending time unwinding there each year for at least two weeks. The rest of the time you can rent it out, which could become a nice income stream."

"He was always thinking of the future," Christina said. "He taught me to think about long-term opportunities too. I'll be your first customer and rent a cabin for a week when you're ready."

"That lake has become quite a lovely place to retreat to," Nelson said. "There's a property manager on-site who can manage rentals for you if you decide to do that. All the details are in your envelopes."

Nelson continued. "He explained to me that he's very proud of both of you, but he worries that you don't take enough time to live at a pace that allows you to appreciate the simple things. This is his wish. He's gifting you the space to stop, listen to God, and balance yourselves."

"He wants me to stay there for two weeks?" Camron asked. "It's hard to break away from a farm for two weeks, even for something right here in town."

"You'll make it work. We find time for what's important. The past few days have proved that. Didn't the two of you adjust your schedules this week without any great sacrifice?"

Eliana's brow lifted, but then she smiled. "You're right. I was wound pretty tight when I first arrived, but then, honestly, I wouldn't change a thing about how this has gone."

Christina held up her hand. "This whole thing with me covering the office was part of the ploy?"

"Afraid so. Your aunt enjoyed the time off. We both did."

"So Johnny was making it so Christina and Eliana would meet?" Camron looked at Eliana. "The timing of your arrival and my weekly chores over at Johnny's put us together too."

Eliana nodded. "I guess so."

"Excellent," Nelson said. "I think we all agree that life can easily become too busy under constraints that we place on ourselves. We'll all do better. On to bigger things. Johnny has split up his property. Let me show you." Nelson rolled out a survey on his desk. "Come look at this."

Camron stood and leaned over the desk. "That's the house, flower farm, pastures. The bridge where we dug up the time capsule is here, and my place is up here."

"Yes, this is the plat as it has been for years. Now…" Nelson put another survey on top of the first. "You can see where he's divided the land. Camron, you now own the pastures and over to the barn. Johnny said you're using that for your cows for calving."

"Correct," said Camron.

"Eliana, your grandfather wants you to have the house and the flower farm."

"Can I sell the house?" Eliana asked. She glanced over at Camron. "I'm not sure I want to. I'm thinking out loud."

Nelson nodded. "You can. It is yours to do with as you wish, but Camron would have the first right of refusal. After that, it's anyone's game."

"Don't sell," Christina said. "I'm not saying that because of the flowers either. Please don't sell. You belong here."

Camron held his tongue. Christina had said what was in his heart.

Nelson handed them each a thick packet stapled at the top. "You can bet your grandfather knew exactly what he wanted to happen. I know you will figure it all out."

"Well, I wish I knew." Eliana's face was red. "I can't just quit my job."

She was noticeably frustrated. She stepped away from the desk and picked up the folder. "Is everything in here?"

"Yes, ma'am." Nelson held her gaze.

"I need some time. I'll get back to you. Please excuse me." She walked out of the room.

"I know Johnny didn't mean to upset her," Camron said.

Nelson rubbed his hand across his forehead. "No. I don't think so. It is a lot to drop on someone at one time though."

"What do we do?" Christina asked, but she didn't wait for an answer. She sprinted out of the office after her new friend.

"Is there anything else I need to know?" Camron asked Nelson.

"No. He's left you two in equitable control of his holdings. Land, a few stocks, and there's some money, as you'll see in the paperwork. I'll distribute that as we get the rest of the deeds and documents transferred over."

"What if she decides to sell?" Camron asked, but he knew Nelson probably had no answer.

"You can buy her out, or you'll get new neighbors. Whatever happens, I'm sure it will all work out fine."

"It'll have to," Camron said. "Thank you for your time."

"Read everything over. We can meet later this week, or whenever is convenient for you."

Camron walked outside, expecting to see Eliana sitting in his truck, but neither she nor Christina were around. He checked the coffee shop then texted her.

ARE YOU OKAY?

I'M SORRY. I NEED TIME. I'M FINE.

NEED A RIDE?

NO. CHRISTINA IS TAKING ME HOME.

Camron's thumbs hovered over the keypad on his phone. He had more he wanted to say. It would have to wait.

All in God's time.

He pushed his hands into his pockets and walked down to the jewelry shop. The electronic bell sounded his arrival. The brightly lit glass cases made the diamonds and gemstones shimmer as if they were animate objects.

"Mr. Carter. I was just going to call you. I was able to do exactly as you asked."

He hadn't expected that. "You already finished it?"

"I did. It was such an interesting project I couldn't wait to give it a try. I think it turned out beautifully." The goldsmith opened a black velvet box.

"It's perfect," Camron said. "Absolutely perfect."

Chapter Eighteen

Eliana had let Christina take her back to the house. She had no idea what she was supposed to do with all of this. Her head swirled with details, and her life just last week was in complete contrast to what she felt right now.

She got in her car and drove north for an hour. The weather was pleasing, and there was beauty everywhere in central Virginia. She stopped at a pull-off in Buchanan County. Standing there looking over the valley, she could see for miles. *If only my future was so easy to picture.*

She took out her phone to call Jan and check to see how things were going in the office.

No signal.

She put her phone back into her pocket. Work shouldn't be her knee-jerk response every time she got stressed. She looked at the clouds and took a long, slow breath. Then she prayed. She asked for guidance. For clear direction, because there were a lot of things showering down on her that conflicted with her current path. Blessings, for sure, but they left her dizzy and afraid to make a misstep. Back at her car, she grabbed a bottle of water from the tote bag in the rear seat.

She hiked over to sit on the rock ledge. Another car, carrying a family of four, pulled over, and they got out to stretch their legs.

The little boy, probably nine or ten years old, kept jumping off the ledge. The dad took pictures of the son's antics.

"Would you like me to take a picture of you all?" she called to them.

"Would you?" The mother walked over to her. "I'd appreciate that. I'm terrible at selfies, so we are hardly ever in a picture together."

Eliana took the mom's phone, and the family posed for the picture. She took a few and then said, "Funny faces this time!"

They all mugged for the camera. "Say 'Blue Ridge Parkway'!"

"Blue Ridge Parkway," they sang out.

Eliana returned the woman's phone. "I hope they turned out."

"I'm sure they did. Thanks. You made my day."

You made my day. It struck Eliana. "You made mine more special too. Thanks for letting me be a small part of yours."

They all piled back into their SUV and headed on their way.

She sat there until the sun began to sink and the spring air cooled. Mist settled along the ridges and knobs across the Blue Ridge Mountains, casting a beautiful silhouette of purples and blues.

It would be dark soon. A bird swooped down next to her on the ledge. Dark bluish gray with a lighter belly, it was a chubby fellow. He didn't make a peep. Just landed and huddled only a few feet from her.

"You don't seem to have a worry in the world." Eliana reached her hand toward the bird.

It cocked its head and took a single hop in her direction.

"My grandfather says I need to slow down. Is it possible to work so hard that you end up with no memories at all?"

The bird cocked its head again.

"I know you work hard. I bet you have a nest nearby. Maybe some baby birds you're taking care of?" Eliana looked over her shoulder. "I guess I should get going. I don't have any babies at home. Really don't have much of anything. Not even a goldfish. I've saved up a lot of money, but I'm not sure what I'm supposed to do with it except save it for retirement."

The bird flew off.

"Yeah. It sounds stupid when you say it out loud." She got up and walked back to her car. Her stomach growled. She'd gone all day without anything to eat. She drove down the parkway and took the first exit with lights.

She pulled over at the next intersection to figure out how far from Burnt Chimney she was. It was only about a thirty-minute drive, so she decided to get dinner while she was here in Roanoke and there were plenty of options.

Up the road, she turned into the parking lot of an Italian restaurant.

The hostess greeted her. "One tonight?"

"Yes. Thank you."

"Right this way."

Eliana followed her to a small two-topper near the salad bar. She looked at the menu, trying to decide what to get. The word of the day seemed to be *decisions*.

"Know what you want, sweetie?" a tall, dark-haired waitress asked.

"I'm just passing through. What do you suggest?"

An older woman sitting with her husband at the next table leaned over. "The pizza. This place has the best pizza in three counties."

"Thank you," Eliana said. "I guess I'll have a slice of pizza then."

"Wait a minute," the woman said. "Honey, are you eating alone? No, you come and help us eat our pizza. We can't possibly eat it all by ourselves. Come. Sit. I won't take no for an answer."

"I'm fine. Really."

"I won't hear of it. Come on. Right, Charles?"

The man smiled at Eliana. "She's not going to give up. Take my word for it. I've been married to her for nearly forty years. You might as well come take a seat."

"Thirty-eight years," the woman corrected him.

Eliana laughed. The waitress put her pen on the pad. "Like he said, you might as well join them. She's right. They never finish their pizza. They're in here every week. Nice folks."

"Well, how do I refuse?"

"You don't," all three of them said.

She got up and sat down at their table. "This is very kind of you."

"No one should ever have to eat alone. I don't think it's good for the digestion," the woman said.

"Then I'm in trouble, because I eat alone most of the time."

The woman looked appalled. "Why? Don't tell me you don't have a husband at home."

"No ma'am. Never married. My job keeps me on the road a lot." Eliana felt like she needed to explain.

"What's a lot?"

"About 75 percent of the time."

"You sound like my husband here. He's not on the road, but he works all the time. This is Charles, and I'm Susan. He's the workaholic. I've been hounding him for two years to take time off and travel like he promised we would."

"You must love what you do, Charles," Eliana said, trying to lighten the mood.

"Not really. It's hard to get out of the practice and leave all your patients to someone else when you've spent your whole life building it. What did you say your name was?"

"Oh, I'm sorry. I'm Eliana. I'm only in town for a couple more days. I'm staying in Burnt Chimney."

"What a small world," Susan said. "That's where we live. Charles has offices in Rocky Mount and here in Roanoke. We rotate. He's brought in some other dentists to keep up with all our patients."

"Wait…" Eliana wondered what the odds were of these two people being Camron's parents.

"Eliana?" Charles said. "Are you the Turner girl?"

"I am. Yes." Eliana squirmed in her seat, wishing the waitress would bring her some water.

"So sorry about your grandfather's passing. It was a beautiful service. I knew you looked familiar when you came in."

What were the odds? Even thirty miles down the road, she was surrounded by people who loved her grandfather.

The waitress set four glasses of water on the table. "Your pizza's on the way."

"Thank you," Susan said. "What is it you do for a living, Eliana?"

"I work for a company that owns hundreds of boutiques across the country. I go in and refresh and stage them for improved profitability. It involves reevaluating the inventory based on previous sales, bringing in new product, and training the staff. We like to refresh each store on a three-year cycle. Some require a complete grand reopening, which takes a few weeks' preparation."

"That's so interesting," Susan said. "But I can't imagine living out of a suitcase. Do you go back home on the weekends?"

"Usually I stay in the town where the store is from start to finish. Anywhere from five days to three weeks. I try to get a couple of days at home between trips."

"My goodness. No wonder you've never been married."

The waitress brought plates and then came back with the pizza platter. "One large sausage, pepperoni, and mushroom pizza. Extra sauce."

"That does look good," said Eliana.

"You're going to love it." Susan put a piece on each of their plates. Then she reached across the table and grabbed her husband's hand and Eliana's. "I'll say the prayer."

Eliana bowed her head.

Susan said, "Heavenly Father, thank You for bringing this young lady across our path tonight. Who knew we had small-town connections? Please bless this food to nourish our bodies and help us all be good disciples of Your Word. Show us Your will, so that we may please You. God bless this food, our families, and friends. In Your name, we pray. Amen."

"Amen," Charles and Eliana said, and another voice joined in too.

"There you are. Late again," Charles said with a hint of sarcasm.

Eliana looked up. "Camron?"

"How did you end up in Roanoke with my parents?"

"Would you believe completely by accident?"

He looked at his mother, who nodded. "It's true. She was going to eat alone. I insisted she join us. I had no idea that she was Johnny

Turner's granddaughter until after we got to talking. Small world. That's what it is," she said.

"Pretty much that," Eliana said.

"Good. I was worried about you." He leaned toward her as he sat down.

"I'm sorry. I just needed some time."

"It's all good news. Not losing Johnny, of course, but what he's trying to do is from the right place in his heart. You have options, and there's no hurry to act on any of it."

"What's going on?" Charles asked.

"It's a long story," Camron said.

Charles didn't seem interested in exploring it further anyway. He changed the subject to the music playing.

They ate, but the conversation wasn't as casual once Camron arrived.

Charles and Susan insisted on paying for the dinner tab, despite Eliana's protests.

Camron's parents walked out ahead of them, and she stood by her car with Camron. "I am sorry I worried you. I'd never want to do that."

"Eliana, I know you're processing a lot of information, but I don't want to miss out on the chance to tell you this. When I thought you might have left for good this morning, it bothered me."

"I won't leave without saying goodbye."

"That's just it. I don't want you to leave at all."

She watched for a smirk or laugh as if he was joking, but there was no punch line.

"Eliana, this might be a schoolboy crush, but I'd hate to never know for sure." He took her hand. "Does it really seem that crazy?"

∽ Chapter Nineteen ∾

Camron widened his stance, worried he might pass out before he got out everything he wanted to say. "Eliana, I'm not married, because I haven't found the right person to share my life with. I want to be married. I want to have children and raise them in Burnt Chimney. I want someone like you."

She stepped back. "But look how my parents ended up. What if I hurt you?"

"You never would. You don't have it in you." He touched her cheek. "Just because your parents didn't stay married doesn't mean all of your relationships are destined to fail. You're special, and you'll find a perfect love. I promise you that. I only hope I might be that person."

"I do wonder what it would be like to have someone in my life," Eliana said. "Someone to talk to when my heart is hurting." She sucked in a breath. "Like it is now."

"I'm here for you."

"You've been a godsend this week. My life is in a rut big enough for a dump truck. I need four-wheel drive to get out of this."

"You know, I've got a truck."

"It's not that simple."

"It can be," he said. "What if it's not a rut, but just the wrong job? You have options now. You have no overhead and a cut flower farm waiting for you, which was designed straight from your child-hood dream. And, I might add, that farm is already making a profit. What do you have to lose?"

"It's just so much."

"You'd be crazy not to take this chance that Johnny has given you. If you hate it, if it's not a fit, you can pack up and leave. You wouldn't have any trouble getting a job. Take a six-month leave of absence as a test run."

Her eyes narrowed as she actually considered it. "I could do that. It certainly would reduce the risk."

"Please, don't make a hasty decision. There's something here between us, and I know Christina thinks you belong here too. Our work is an important part of sustaining the future of this town. It's where your father grew up. We can give back to this community. Grow with it."

"Okay, okay. I need to breathe, but I'm hearing you. I promise."

"Thank you for listening."

"How could I not?" She squeezed his hand. "You're pretty awe-some, Camron Carter. My life is totally topsy-turvy at this moment. I feel so off-balance that I'm honestly not sure if I'm flying on the wings of angels, or drowning."

"Follow me back, okay?"

"Sure."

He got in his truck and pulled out into traffic, being careful not to lose her in his rear-view mirror. He didn't turn off on the road to his house. Instead he drove all the way to Johnny's doorstep.

Eliana got out of her car. "You didn't have to do that."

He walked over to her. "I know, but I want you to know I'll go the extra mile for you. Always. And that's a promise, even as friends."

"Be careful what you promise. If I decide to stay, I've got stuff in California that'll need to get moved. That's more than a mile or two."

"An adventure. I've never seen California. I could be persuaded."

She stood there and looked around, taking in a deep breath of the country air. "I do love it here."

"Your grandfather said to me on more than one occasion that sometimes, in the middle of an ordinary life, love will fall into place and create a fairy tale."

"He used to say that to me too," Eliana said. "I thought that was the most ridiculous idea I'd ever heard, but now I feel like I'm living in the fairy tale."

Camron gave her a slow smile. "And is that so bad?"

Eliana's heart beat wildly. She whispered, "This is crazy."

"Is it? Who's to say what's crazy? I think this…what we're feel-ing…is worth the risk. Is it crazy to believe in something amazingly special?"

"We haven't spoken in years until now. We barely know each other."

"We know the very heart of each other. The foundation of who we are. Our beginnings and the paths we've traveled. That has to mean something. I don't want you to leave."

Eliana pressed her lips together. "I want to believe it could be true, to find out what might be possible, but I'm afraid."

"It's okay to be afraid."

She clenched her fist, wishing she was braver, praying for some sign that this wasn't all a dream but truly God's plan.

"I want to give you something. Can you wait here one second?"

"I'm not going anywhere."

He jogged over to his truck and came back with something in his hand. "Okay. Come up here on the porch."

She followed him and took the key from under the milk can to open the door. She turned and smiled. "If I lived here, I'd move that."

"You should. Everyone knows where it is."

"Mom would never let me have a dog. I could get a chocolate Lab maybe."

"They are great dogs. There are so many possibilities ahead of you."

She relaxed as all those dreams seemed within reach.

"I know how you've always wondered about that cuff link on the mantel," he said.

"Yeah. So much so that I couldn't keep my hands off of it now that Grandpa Johnny is gone, and what did I do? Lost it, or it got stolen. I feel horrible about it."

"Well, you can stop that right now."

"I wish. That's easy to say and hard to do. You know how much it meant to him."

He took a small bag from his pocket and handed it to her.

"This is for me?"

"Yes. Custom. One-of-a-kind, like you. I hope you love it."

She dumped the contents of the bag into her hand. The delicate gold chain sparkled. She pressed her finger and thumb to the beautiful pendant. Smooth on one side, with the scrolling *ET* on the back. "Is this—?"

"It wasn't stolen, Eliana. I took it the morning I was there for your grilled peanut butter, apple, and honey sandwiches. I'd hoped you wouldn't notice, but I'd already taken it to the jeweler by the time you discovered it missing. I'm sorry. I should have told you, but I had the idea after I saw you looking at the love tokens in the antique shop, and then you were so touched by the romance of your grandfather's gift to your grandmother that I wanted to do something for you."

"This is so thoughtful." She pressed her lips together. "Does it have some kind of significance?"

"I sure hope so. Originally, I was just making a token for you, because we were friends, but then I realized I was, am, still in love with you, and I don't want you to leave, and the only way I know to get that across is with this."

He took a knee. "I had the jeweler in town turn it into a love token. For you."

Her jaw dropped. The *ET*, the intricate scrolling, it was all there. "My goodness. It's beautiful."

"It's quick. I'm aware of that, and it doesn't have to be a marriage proposal, but how about a proposal of love? One that means we'll see where this will take us, because I know that we're soulmates."

She nodded.

"Can I fasten it for you?"

"Yes." She turned her back to him and lifted her hair from her shoulders. She could feel his fingers shaking at the nape of her neck.

"I got it. Turn around and let me see."

She pivoted toward him, her hand touching the love token. "How does it look?"

"Beautiful. A little less beautiful than you, but it's perfect." He paused. "Eliana, is there even a glimmer of hope for a man like me in your life?"

She nodded, more certain about this place than she could have ever imagined. "More than a glimmer. I feel like I've come home."

"You forgive me for borrowing the cuff link and letting you worry? I promise I'll never make you worry again."

"You're forgiven. I'm falling for you too."

"You've got my heart soaring. Johnny, did you hear this?" Camron yelled.

She laughed. "What do we do? I wouldn't want to mess up this friendship. Is it worth the risk?"

"Completely."

She blushed. "There's a lot of heavy stuff coming this week. I have so many decisions to make."

"I'm here for you. I'll help you."

"We can get through it all together."

"You are an angel, and even gold could never outshine you."

Eliana went into his arms. "Whatever happens, the silver lining, or gold in this case, is that we now know that even a single cuff link isn't useless."

Dear Reader,

We had so much fun exploring Burnt Chimney, Virginia! Tucked in the eastern foothills of the Blue Ridge Mountains, this is a stunning part of the country, with its rows and rows of undulations lined up one after another. It's also a place rich with history, where the past is still imprinted on the present. We loved bringing this magical place to life on the page.

Though you can find Burnt Chimney, Virginia, listed on maps, these days it's little more than a crossroads, with a historical marker to show where the chimney—and Nannie Starkey Turner's store—once stood. Rocky Mount, the nearby town where much of both stories takes place, is a charming old village with a thriving downtown and a historic train depot, though this depot was built too late to be the one where Everett Turner works in the historical story.

Once we realized why Burnt Chimney was called that—learning there really had been a store there and it had burned down, leaving only the blackened chimney behind—it wasn't hard to decide on the mystery for the historical section of the book. Who set fire to Nannie's store, and why? Unraveling that mystery, that small piece of history, leads to the place we call Burnt Chimney today.

The history of a town has a way of evolving as people add their own experiences and interpretations, and sometimes it's forgotten altogether. Can one tiny connection that altered the past also change the future? Those were the questions we wanted to answer as we took you on a modern-day look of this small town. Today, Burnt

Chimney, more commonly known as Wirtz, has a population less than five thousand and only a few businesses, pushing the purchasing habits to the neighboring town of Rocky Mount or city of Roanoke just a thirty-minute drive away.

Join us in exploring Burnt Chimney and its residents who are as alive and colorful as the beautiful mountains of Virginia.

We hope you've enjoyed reading these stories as much as we enjoyed writing them.

Best,

Beth Adams and Nancy Naigle

About the Authors

Beth Adams

Beth Adams lives in Brooklyn, New York, with her husband and two young daughters. When she's not writing, she spends her time cleaning up after two devious cats and trying to find time to read mysteries.

Nancy Naigle

Nancy Naigle lives in Patrick Springs, Virginia, in the Blue Ridge Mountains. She balances her time between writing and family and spending time with friends, antiquing, crafting, and enjoying the occasional spa day.

STORY BEHIND THE NAME

Burnt Chimney, Virginia

Burnt Chimney, Virginia, is listed on most maps, but it isn't a town in any real sense. It's actually more of a crossroads—one that for many years was dominated by a charred chimney. At the corner of Routes 116 and 122, just outside of Rocky Mount, there is a plaque that reads:

Burnt Chimney

1885–1891

Nannie Starkey Turner built a store near this site in 1886. Later it burned, leaving the chimney standing. It also served as a post office named Reverie and was operated by Stephen C. Kennett. It ceased operating in 1891. Later the location became known as Burnt Chimney by many Franklin County natives and is now a landmark.

In our historical story, Nannie doesn't build her store in 1886. She opens it in 1890, and we left out the post office details. Though we've done our best to stay true to the history as far as we know it, we've taken some liberties with the facts to try to bring you a satisfying story.

Burnt Chimney is still small in size and big in heart. A peaceful cut-through, most travelers passing through are on their way to Smith Mountain Lake, known as western Virginia's biggest playground and Virginia's second-largest lake.

Johnny Pops

You're going to love Grandpa Johnny's popover recipe. These light and airy muffins are crispy on the outside with a soft, buttery, and slightly eggy flavor. Popovers are impressive but easy to make.

Ingredients:

1¼ cups whole milk (You can't skimp on the fat here or these just won't rise the way they're supposed to.)

1 tablespoon butter, melted and cooled

1 cup all-purpose flour

¼ teaspoon salt

2 large eggs

Directions:

1. Let your eggs and milk come to room temperature for about 30 minutes before getting started. This tiny detail will ensure you get that airy puff to your popover that we all love!

2. While you watch the clock, use that time to preheat your oven to 450° and butter up your muffin tin.

3. Once we're all warmed up, in a small bowl, beat milk, butter, flour, and salt until blended.

4. Add 1 egg at a time, beating well after each addition.

5. Fill your buttered muffin pan wells about 3/4 full. Don't over-fill, because these are going to rise to new heights!

6. Bake for 15 minutes.

7. Reduce heat to 350° and bake until the outside of your popovers are nice and crispy. This should take about 20 minutes longer.

8. Remove from oven and prick each popover with a sharp knife to allow steam to escape.

9. Serve immediately with butter and jam, or go savory with herbal cream cheese.

10. Enjoy this little taste of Burnt Chimney's dear Johnny Turner.

Read on for a sneak peek of the first book in an exciting
new mystery series from Guideposts Books—
Whistle Stop Café Mysteries!

UNDER THE APPLE TREE
by GABRIELLE MEYER

Dust motes floated on the warm, thick air as Debbie Albright shoved a cardboard box into the corner of her attic. A sneeze started to build in her nose, forcing her to stop what she was doing and hold her hand above her lip. Her eyes watered, but the feeling soon passed.

"Your allergies will never survive this move." Janet Shaw, Debbie's best friend, tossed her a box of tissues. "Should we take a break? The coffee shop has half-priced mochas on Saturdays."

Debbie pulled a tissue free. "We don't have time for a break. I want to get all the storage boxes out of the living room before Ian gets here with the furniture." He would be arriving any minute, and Debbie and Janet still had several more trips to make up the two flights of stairs to the attic.

The air was hot and stuffy, and a hundred years' worth of dust lined the cracks and crevices of the old shiplap on the ceiling and walls. Beneath her feet, the boards creaked in protest, reminding Debbie that the home was old and she had a big job ahead of her. But she couldn't be happier or more excited to finally be back in Dennison, Ohio. The beautiful craftsman-style bungalow she had purchased would need quite a bit of work, but she wasn't afraid to tackle the project, especially with her friends' help.

"It looks like Mr. Zink left a few treasures for you," Janet commented. The lid on an old trunk creaked in protest as she lifted it.

"He mentioned that his nieces and nephews left a few odds and ends." Debbie shoved the used tissue into the pocket of her overalls as she moved around several boxes to join Janet. "But he said most of it would probably need to be thrown away."

"This looks like it's full of old newspapers." Janet bent down and lifted one from the trunk, her blue eyes opening wide. "This is from December, 1941."

Debbie took the paper from Janet and slipped one of her brown curls back into the bandanna tied around her head. Despite the heat, a chill climbed up her spine as she read the headline. "'War Declared.'" Even though it had happened before her lifetime, she still felt a keen tug in her heart when she thought about World War II. "I can't even imagine what it would have been like to live through such a difficult time."

Janet lifted more newspapers out of the trunk. "Some of these are from the *Dennison Daily Transcript* and talk about all the troops coming through the depot."

"I could read these for hours."

Janet stood up straight. "We'll have to go through all this later."

"I probably won't have much free time, even after I'm settled." Not with all the work she had to do on the house and the plans they had to open the Whistle Stop Café in the old train depot a few blocks up the street. After leaving her corporate job in Cleveland, Debbie had come back to town to do just that. Somehow, she'd convinced Janet to help her, knowing what an amazing cook and baker her best friend had become over the years. Janet had worked for the Third Street Bakery for much of her career and was ready to start her own business. Their grand opening would be in three weeks, which meant they still had a massive amount of work ahead of them.

As Debbie lowered the newspaper back into the trunk, something else caught her attention. "What's this?"

An olive-green metal box with the stenciled words Special Services, US Army sat at the bottom of the trunk. Leather straps on the sides made it easy for Debbie to lift out, but they were stiff and cracked with age. She was afraid they would break.

Janet watched as Debbie set the metal box on the dusty floor.

"It's definitely military issue, whatever it is." Debbie ran her fingers along the stenciled words. Iron corner protectors and rivets lined the seams, while clasps held the top and bottom together. "And it's old," she added.

"I bet it's from the 1940s, like the newspapers." Janet squatted next to Debbie. "Do you think it belonged to Mr. Zink?"

"I'm sure it did. He was an infantryman during the war. He fought in Europe and came home to tell about it."

"Do you think he meant to leave it when he moved?" Janet leaned over to inspect the side of the box.

"I don't know." Debbie unhooked the clasps and gently pulled upward. The hinges groaned, but the box held a wonderful surprise. "It's a portable phonograph!"

"I didn't even know there was such a thing way back then."

The phonograph was in great shape for its age. "Who would ever guess that such an ugly box could house such a beautiful instrument?"

"Do you know how it works?"

Debbie had seen one similar to it in an antique store once, and the owner had shown her how it worked, but the one she'd seen had been in a lot worse shape. "If I remember correctly…" She lifted a handle from the bottom left-hand corner and inserted it into the front of the box. It was curved, and she used it to crank the mechanism. When it was tight, she reached up and shifted a lever, and the turntable began to spin.

"Amazing!" Janet's voice held awe. "I can't believe it still works."

"These things are worth a lot of money," Debbie said. "I need to let Mr. Zink know he forgot to take it."

"Do you think maybe…" Janet rose and went back to the trunk where she moved the rest of the newspapers. "Bingo!" She lifted a thin cardboard sheath.

Debbie smiled as she took the small record. The label in the center had a handwritten note on it, which she read out loud. "'To Ray, with love, Eleanor.'" Under that was the song title, "Don't Sit Under the Apple Tree (With Anyone Else but Me)."

Janet stared at the record. "Do you think Ray is Mr. Zink?"

Debbie nodded. "His first name is Raymond." She flipped off the turntable and let it come to a stop and then set the record on it before pushing the lever again. Her heart pounded as she lifted the needle and gently set it on the record, hoping she knew what she was doing. The last thing she wanted to do was damage the record or the phonograph.

The noise was scratchy at first, and then a clear, beautiful voice filled the attic, singing a version of the Andrews Sisters' popular song.

Debbie looked up and met Janet's surprised gaze. "Who do you think Eleanor was?"

"Whoever she was, she had a great voice."

"This sounds like an amateur recording," Debbie said. "I wonder if she was Mr. Zink's sweetheart."

"He never got married, did he?" Janet asked. "I wonder what happened to Eleanor."

Debbie perked up when she heard a noise from downstairs. "It sounds like Ian is here."

Janet sighed. "I was hoping we could listen to the other records in the trunk." She shrugged. "There'll be time later, I suppose."

Debbie lifted the needle and switched off the turntable. As Janet rose and went to the stairs to greet her husband, Debbie gently slid the record back into its sheath.

Mr. Zink must have forgotten that the phonograph and records were in the attic. It didn't seem right to keep them from him. As soon as she had a bit of free time, she'd stop by the assisted-living home and ask him what he wanted her to do with the trunk.

It would give her a chance to visit with the elderly man again and give him an update on her big move. He'd always been one of her favorite people, full of fun stories and interesting historical tidbits about Dennison. She would take any excuse she could find to stop in and visit.

The portable phonograph, not to mention Eleanor's record, was the perfect reason.

The next day, Debbie had a few minutes after church to stop in and visit Raymond Zink. He had moved into the Good Shepherd Retirement Center a couple of months earlier, after deciding to sell his home to Debbie. She was familiar with the Good Shepherd, since her dad had recently retired from managing the facility.

Debbie passed through the front doors and into the cozy foyer. The sitting room was full of residents and their families, and she smiled at several people she knew. Though she hadn't lived in Dennison for almost twenty years, she had come home often and stayed in touch with many of her childhood friends and their family members. It was comforting to return to her old church, see her former schoolteachers downtown, run into an old neighbor at the grocery store, and generally feel at home again. Cleveland had never felt so tight-knit or full of a sense of community. At least, not in the same way as her hometown.

Debbie stopped at the front desk with the record and phonograph. A volunteer sat there with a smile on his face.

"Good afternoon," he said. "I'm Steven. How can I help you?"

"Hi, Steven." Debbie returned his smile. "I'm looking for Raymond Zink."

"Ray?" Steven's grin widened. "He's holding court in the dining room this afternoon."

"Holding court?"

Steven shook his head as he chuckled. "You'll see. Dining room is that way and to the left." He pointed in the direction she should go.

"Thank you. Mind if I leave this phonograph here? It belongs to Mr. Zink, but it's a little heavy to haul around."

"Sure. I'll have someone take it to Ray's room for you, if you'd like."

"That would be great." She smiled as she walked down the hall, following the smell of pot roast and baked bread.

Even before she turned the corner into the dining room, she could hear Mr. Zink's voice. It was loud and clear, and he was telling the story of Old Bing, the service dog that had gone to war with the Gray brothers of Dennison in June of 1918.

Debbie stopped inside the doorway and listened as Mr. Zink continued his story. He sat in his wheelchair, near the upright piano, one of his hands resting on the ivory keys, as if he'd just finished playing a song. He was famous in Dennison for his piano playing.

Sitting around him were about a dozen people. Some looked like they were residents, while others appeared to be visiting family members. Mr. Zink held everyone's attention, from the youngest to the oldest.

"Bing was only nine days old when he was smuggled onto a troop ship by the Gray brothers, one hundred and five years ago this month," Mr. Zink said. "He went through basic training and served in active duty, with fifty-eight days in the trenches, and received two citations for bravery." Mr. Zink's body showed his advanced age, but his eyes lit up and his voice was strong as he spoke. "Old Bing survived being gassed twice and came back to Dennison with yellow teeth and patches of missing fur from the side effects. But for his service in the First World War, he received the regular sixty-eight-dollar bonus for discharged soldiers."

Debbie had heard the story of Old Bing before, but she never tired of it. When Mr. Zink saw her standing there, his face brightened with a smile and he excused himself from his audience to join her, pushing the wheels on his chair.

"Hello, Debbie. It's so nice to see you again."

"Hello, Mr. Zink." Debbie knew him from growing up in her church. When she decided to come back to Dennison to open the Whistle Stop Café, he heard she was looking for a house and offered his. It was almost miraculous how everything had fallen into place. "I'm happy to see you've found a new audience to share your passion for history."

"I won't stop until the Good Lord takes me home." He motioned to a chair. "First of all, everyone here calls me Ray. Second, have a seat and tell me why you're here. I hope everything is okay at the house."

"It's perfect. I love it." She set her bag down and pulled out the old record inside its sheath. "I actually came by to let you know there was a trunk left in the attic and I thought you might want it."

"A trunk?" Ray squinted. "What was in it?"

"Some newspapers, a portable phonograph, which is being delivered to your room, and this." She handed him the record.

Ray looked at it for a moment and then slowly slipped the record out of the sheath. His mouth began to quiver, and his gaze seemed to slip back in time. "My Eleanor." Finally, he looked at Debbie. "Where did you say you found this?"

"In an old trunk in the attic," she repeated, watching him closely. "I thought maybe you had forgotten it."

"I hadn't forgotten—how could I forget about her?" He held the record to his chest. "I haven't been able to get into that attic for almost a decade, and I was sure I'd lost this. I can't believe you found it."

"Who was she?" Debbie asked. "She had a beautiful singing voice."

"It was only a small part of her beauty." Tears filled Ray's eyes as he spoke. "I've never known a woman like Eleanor O'Reilly before or since."

"Was she your sweetheart?"

"She was more than that. She was my very heart and soul." He looked at the record again and tenderly ran his hand over the label. "She was supposed to be my wife."

"What happened to her?" Debbie asked.

He shook his head. "I don't know."

Debbie frowned. "You don't know?"

"When I left Dennison to join the army, she was standing on the platform at the depot to see me off. She promised to write and told me that when I returned, we'd be married." He swallowed and let out a sad sigh. "But her letters stopped abruptly, and when I came home, she wasn't here. I looked for her for months, but I never saw her again. I eventually came to the realization that she didn't love me. It was the only explanation I could come to." He was quiet for a moment, lost in his own thoughts. "I never loved again."

Debbie's heart broke for Ray. She had lost her fiancé when he died in Afghanistan as a special forces officer. It had been years, but sometimes it felt like yesterday. Would the pain remain with her as long as it had with Ray? The thought felt weighty and suffocating.

"Debbie?" Ray asked.

"Yes?"

"Would you help me find Eleanor? She probably doesn't want to hear from me, if she's still alive, but I've always wondered where she went and how she made out. It would do my heart good to know she was happy."

Debbie smiled. Though she had a house to remodel and a restaurant to open in less than three weeks, how could she say no to such a heartfelt request? "I'd love to help you."

His lips trembled, but his smile was radiant. "Can I tell you how I met Eleanor?" he asked.

Debbie couldn't wait to find out.

A Note from the Editors

We hope you enjoyed another book in the Love's a Mystery series, published by Guideposts. For over seventy-five years Guideposts, a nonprofit organization, has been driven by a vision of a world filled with hope. We aspire to be the voice of a trusted friend, a friend who makes you feel more hopeful and connected.

By making a purchase from Guideposts, you join our community in touching millions of lives, inspiring them to believe that all things are possible through faith, hope, and prayer. Your continued support allows us to provide uplifting resources to those in need. Whether through our online communities, websites, apps, or publications, we strive to inspire our audiences, bring them together, comfort, uplift, entertain, and guide them.

To learn more, please go to guideposts.org.

Find inspiration, find faith, find Guideposts.

Shop our best sellers and favorites at

guideposts.org/shop

Or scan the QR code to go directly
to our Shop

SAVANNAH SECRETS

Welcome to Savannah, Georgia, a picture-perfect Southern city known for its manicured parks, moss-covered oaks, and antebellum architecture. Walk down one of the cobblestone streets, and you'll come upon Magnolia Investigations. It is here where two friends have joined forces to unravel some of Savannah's deepest secrets. Tag along as clues are exposed, red herrings discarded, and thrilling surprises revealed. Find inspiration in the special bond between Meredith Bellefontaine and Julia Foley. Cheer the friends on as they listen to their hearts and rely on their faith to solve each new case that comes their way.

The Hidden Gate
The Fallen Petal
Double Trouble
Whispering Bells
Where Time Stood Still
The Weight of Years

Willful Transgressions
Season's Meetings
Southern Fried Secrets
The Greatest of These
Patterns of Deception
The Waving Girl
Beneath a Dragon Moon
Garden Variety Crimes
Meant for Good
A Bone to Pick
Honeybees & Legacies
True Grits
Sapphire Secret
Jingle Bell Heist
Buried Secrets
A Puzzle of Pearls
Facing the Facts
Resurrecting Trouble
Forever and a Day

MYSTERIES OF MARTHA'S VINEYARD

∾⦿⦿∾

Priscilla Latham Grant has inherited a lighthouse! So with not much more than a strong will and a sore heart, the recent widow says good-bye to her lifelong Kansas home and heads to the quaint and historic island of Martha's Vineyard, Massachusetts. There, she comes face-to-face with adventures, which include her trusty canine friend, Jake, three delightful cousins she didn't know she had, and Gerald O'Bannon, a handsome Coast Guard captain—plus head-scratching mysteries that crop up with surprising regularity.

A Light in the Darkness
Like a Fish Out of Water
Adrift
Maiden of the Mist
Making Waves
Don't Rock the Boat
A Port in the Storm
Thicker Than Water
Swept Away
Bridge Over Troubled Waters

LOVE'S A MYSTERY

Smoke on the Water
Shifting Sands
Shark Bait
Seascape in Shadows
Storm Tide
Water Flows Uphill
Catch of the Day
Beyond the Sea
Wider Than an Ocean
Sheeps Passing in the Night
Sail Away Home
Waves of Doubt
Lifeline
Flotsam & Jetsam
Just Over the Horizon

MIRACLES & MYSTERIES OF MERCY HOSPITAL

Four talented women from very different walks of life witness the miracles happening around them at Mercy Hospital and soon become fast friends. Join Joy Atkins, Evelyn Perry, Anne Mabry, and Shirley Bashore as, together, they solve the puzzling mysteries that arise at this Charleston, South Carolina, historic hospital— rumored to be under the protection of a guardian angel. Come along as our quartet of faithful friends solve mysteries, stumble upon a few of the hospital's hidden and forgotten passageways, and discover historical treasures along the way! This fast-paced series is filled with inspiration, adventure, mystery, delightful humor, and loads of Southern charm!

Where Mercy Begins
Prescription for Mystery
Angels Watching Over Me
A Change of Art
Conscious Decisions
Surrounded by Mercy
Broken Bonds

Mercy's Healing
To Heal a Heart
A Cross to Bear
Merciful Secrecy
Sunken Hopes
Hair Today, Gone Tomorrow
Pain Relief
Redeemed by Mercy
A Genius Solution
A Hard Pill to Swallow
Ill at Ease
'Twas the Clue Before Christmas

Find more inspiring stories in these best-loved Guideposts fiction series!

Mysteries of Lancaster County

Follow the Classen sisters as they unravel clues and uncover hidden secrets in Mysteries of Lancaster County. As you get to know these women and their friends, you'll see how God brings each of them together for a fresh start in life.

Secrets of Wayfarers Inn

Retired schoolteachers find themselves owners of an old warehouse-turned-inn that is filled with hidden passages, buried secrets, and stunning surprises that will set them on a course to puzzling mysteries from the Underground Railroad.

Tearoom Mysteries Series

Mix one stately Victorian home, a charming lakeside town in Maine, and two adventurous cousins with a passion for tea and hospitality. Add a large scoop of intriguing mystery, and sprinkle generously with faith, family, and friends, and you have the recipe for *Tearoom Mysteries*.

Ordinary Women of the Bible

Richly imagined stories—based on facts from the Bible—have all the plot twists and suspense of a great mystery, while bringing you fascinating insights on what it was like to be a woman living in the ancient world.

To learn more about these books, visit Guideposts.org/Shop